Working with Young Women

by the same author

Working with Young Men
Activities for Exploring Personal, Social and Emotional Issues
2nd Edition
Vanessa Rogers
ISBN 978 1 84905 101 9

of related interest

Helping Adolescents and Adults to Build Self-Esteem
A Photocopiable Resource Book
Deborah M. Plummer
ISBN 978 1 84310 185 7

Feeling Like Crap
Young People and the Meaning of Self-Esteem
Nick Luxmoore
ISBN 978 1 84310 682 1

Street Wise
A Programme for Educating Young People about
Citizenship, Rights, Responsibilities and the Law
Sam Frankel
Foreword by Bishop Tim Stevens
ISBN 978 1 84310 680 7

What Have I Done?
A Victim Empathy Programme for Young People
Pete Wallis
With Clair Aldington and Marian Liebmann
Illustrated by Emily Wallis
ISBN 978 1 84310 979 2

Working with Gangs and Young People
A Toolkit for Resolving Group Conflict
Jessie Feinstein and Nia Imani Kuumba
ISBN 978 1 84310 447 6

Working with Anger and Young People
Nick Luxmoore
ISBN 978 1 84310 466 7

Understanding Drug Issues
A Photocopiable Resource Workbook
2nd Edition
David Emmett and Graeme Nice
ISBN 978 1 84310 350 9

Getting Wise to Drugs
A Resource for Teaching Children about Drugs, Dangerous
Substances and Other Risky Situations
David Emmett and Graeme Nice
ISBN 978 1 84310 507 7

Working with Young Women

Second Edition

Activities for Exploring Personal, Social and Emotional Issues

Vanessa Rogers

Jessica Kingsley Publishers
London and Philadelphia

First published in 2006 by the National Youth Agency

Second edition published in 2010
by Jessica Kingsley Publishers
116 Pentonville Road
London N1 9JB, UK
and
400 Market Street, Suite 400
Philadelphia, PA 19106, USA

www.jkp.com

Library of Congress Cataloging in Publication Data
A CIP catalog record for this book is available from the Library of Congress

British Library Cataloguing in Publication Data
A CIP catalogue record for this book is available from the British Library

ISBN 978 1 84905 095 1

Printed and bound in Great Britain by
MPG Books Limited

Contents

Acknowledgements

I would like to thank Donna Lancaster, Ann McKay, Hertfordshire Youth Connexions, Helen Walker (Cambridgeshire Youth Service), Naomi Little (Youth Matters), Carol Hawkes, Gillian Porter, Deborah Mulroney, Joshua Oakes-Rogers (Simon Balle School), Darren Godfrey (Essex Youth Service) and Geoff Fisher (Peterborough Youth Service), all of whose suggestions for activities are included in this book.

Thanks also to any other youth workers or personal advisers not specifically named who have contributed ideas or been a part of the projects mentioned.

About the Author

Vanessa is a qualified teacher and youth worker with a master's degree in Community Education. She has over ten years' experience within the Hertfordshire Youth Service both at practitioner and management levels. Prior to achieving national recognition for her work Vanessa managed a wide range of services for young people including a large youth centre and targeted detached projects for Hertfordshire County Council. She devises and delivers professional development training programmes and writes for *Youth Work Now*. In addition she has been commissioned to devise training packs for a wide range of organisations, including the BBC.

This book is one of 19 resources written by Vanessa to support the development of creative youth work and social education.

Her website www.vanessarogers.co.uk gives detailed information about further titles, training and consultancy visits.

Introduction

For me, work with young women continues to be one of the most important as well as one of the most enjoyable aspects of youth work. It has been great fun to pull together a hugely diverse collection of resources specifically devised to engage, motivate and meet the needs of young women within a single-gender environment.

Using group work, discussions, art and role-play, the book offers ideas to help build self-esteem, confidence and assertiveness skills. Issues considered include body image, positive relationships and peer choices, as well as work around alcohol and healthy lifestyles.

This resource can be used in a wide range of settings, not just confined to the youth club. The suggestions work equally well in schools, pupil referral units, youth offending teams and voluntary sector youth groups. The activities are appropriate for all young women aged 13–19, include suggestions for those who have special educational needs, and allow adaptations for one-to-one work.

This revised 2010 edition of *Working with Young Women* includes additional new resources, updates some of the most popular tried and tested activities and offers a whole new chapter: Chapter 6, 'Gender and Stereotypes'.

Getting started

These are short games and tasks to use at the start of each session to encourage the young women to start working together. Warm-ups are a particularly good way of introducing a topic to a group and to start the process of getting to know each other. You can also use them to break up different sections of your programme and to re-energise the group and move discussions on.

Self-esteem and body image

Looking at body image and encouraging young women to feel good about themselves is important. These activities offer a range of ways to encourage reflection and promote discussion.

To maximise learning, make sure that you have assessed individual need, and that the group is established enough for the young women to feel safe and comfortable sharing and discussing feelings together. Allow plenty of time for these sessions to work through the issues raised, thoroughly.

Make sure you have details of any additional services available in the area, for example youth counselling, so that you can support young women into accessing these if and when appropriate.

Healthy lifestyles

Concerns about young women binge drinking and misusing alcohol are widely publicised. This section offers opportunities to engage young women in looking at alcohol, healthy eating and other health-related issues, giving information, exploring values and building skills to make healthy lifestyle choices.

It also has ideas to offer information about sexual health and sexually transmitted infections and explores the ethics around making choices.

Positive relationships

This section focuses on the complex area of personal relationships, including friendships and family as well as partners.

It is important to review contracts and agreements made within the group before you start. Additionally, this is a good time to reinforce confidentiality boundaries so that the young women are clear.

You may need parental consent before some of the sessions, depending on the age of the young women and the issues you plan to cover. This ensures that parents are informed of the programme and any cultural issues or areas of concern are resolved together.

Gender and stereotypes

This section offers ideas to celebrate womanhood and look at positive role models in a wider context. It will enable young women to start to look at the wider issues for women, including equality in the workplace and gender stereotyping.

Endings

The activities and ideas in this section aim to end your group on a high note and consolidate work done. They encourage the young women to reflect on learning and evaluate the issues they have looked at.

Chapter 1

Setting up a Young Women's Group

Who should come?

Before you start recruiting, review and consider your reasons for setting up the group. Is it a request from young women you are already working with? Or is it to meet a need identified by a partner agency, for example young women who are at risk of early teenage pregnancy? The answer to this will determine your target group. If the group is to be a closed project with a referral process you will need to spend time talking through expectations and agreeing responsibilities with the referring agencies as well as the participants.

If it is to be a drop-in, or open-door policy, then you will need to think about how you are going to promote the group to make sure that young women know the event is taking place. This is particularly an issue if young women are under-represented in your club or project and may involve outreach work in advance of the group starting.

How many?

For group work that aims to look at personal issues, such as body image or relationships, a small group of between 8 and 12 young women is appropriate. You will also need to consider the age, maturity and levels of existing knowledge within the group.

For larger groups you can always split into smaller working groups for issue-based sessions and come together for team-building activities and games.

What will the young women get out of it?

There are plenty of accreditation schemes for informal education in youth work settings (see www.nya.org.uk for more details), so check out which schemes are already licensed to your organisation. These could include AQA (Assessment and Qualifications Alliance), Youth Achievement Awards and the Duke of Edinburgh Award Scheme. Most local authorities have a nominated person for accreditation and they could offer you support.

Develop creative ways to capture Recorded Outcomes, for example using photos, video or social networking, as well as the more traditional paper-based methods. It is important that the young women can see what they have learnt/achieved as a result of your intervention in a way that is meaningful to them.

How will you measure success?

Clear aims and objectives make the evaluation part of any project a whole lot easier! Methods of measuring and evaluating the outcomes of work should be put into place and agreed before any work starts during the planning stages. This should include qualitative methods such as focus groups or anecdotal feedback as well as quantitative methods of recording numbers attending and formal evaluation forms.

Whatever you choose it is important to include the young women in the process so that accreditation, evaluation and reflecting on learning becomes a part of the session and not something that is simply 'done to' them.

Boundaries

Make sure that you are clear and straight with the young women from the first session about where your confidentiality ends. Ensure that both you and they are aware of the boundaries set for the group, and also your legal duty regarding child protection issues. That way everyone knows that you may have a duty to act upon information they give and have a choice about how much they share.

Ground rules

The young women should be encouraged to respect differences within the group, such as sexuality, disability or ethnicity. The group needs to accept that each of them will bring their own experiences of family, friendship and sexual relationships and that no single viewpoint is necessarily right or wrong.

They can then work together to produce a 'contract' or set of ground rules they are happy to work with. This can be flexible but should include things like:

- Racist, sexist or any other discriminatory behaviour will not be tolerated.

- Everyone should be willing to listen to each other.

- Everyone should be willing to participate in group activities.

Finally, you will need to agree what sanctions, if any, will be used if the young women 'break' the contract or behave in an unacceptable way. Depending on their ages you may need to inform parents or teachers, etc. if this includes being sent home or temporary exclusion.

Chapter 2

Getting Started

2.1 Paper game

This warm-up can be used with a large or small group and is appropriate for young women of all ages.

Aim

The aim of the activity is to share information, discover similarities and share differences.

You will need

- a toilet roll or box of tissues
- pens.

How to do it

Seat the young women in a large circle and begin by telling a story. For example:

> 'We are all stranded here in this building and we are going to have to stay the night. I am going to pass around a toilet roll and would like you to take as much off the roll as you think you are going to need for the night!'

Or

> 'We are all going to watch a really sad film – I warn you it is a real tearjerker! I am going to pass a box of tissues around and I want you to take as many tissues as you think you will need for the film!'

You can elaborate on the stories as much as you like, and then pass around the box of tissues or the toilet roll.

Once all the participants have taken some paper hand out pens and tell them that they now have to write something about themselves onto each sheet that they have. This will really vary and usually causes laughter – especially if someone has taken a big handful!

When everyone has finished writing take it in turns around the circle to share what has been written, stopping to discuss or ask questions.

The activity finishes when everyone has shared at least three things about themselves.

2.2   All about us

This is a warm-up to divide the young women into two groups. It can be used with any size of group and is good for mixed ability groups.

Aim

To explore similarities and differences between the young women in the group.

You will need

- nothing!

How to do it

Explain that this activity is all about finding out information about each other, for example things that people like, things that make them laugh, etc.

Invite everyone in the group to the centre of the room. Start off by saying something that is clearly fun, for example, 'If you are more like a BMW, go to the right of the room. If you are more like a Volkswagen Beetle, go to the left of the room.' Make sure that you stress that there are no value judgements attached to these choices – it is all about personal preference!

For groups that are not mobile, invite the young women to raise or lower a hand to show their choices.

Once the group has separated, invite everyone to see who is standing near them, indicating shared interests. Then ask the young women to look across the room to see who has different thoughts. Repeat the activity as many times as you want, pausing to discuss as appropriate.

The final round will divide the group into two groups in which to work on the next activity.

Ideas

- Winter/Summer
- Ocean/River
- Cat/Dog
- Pizza/Salad
- Book/Film

2.3   Assumptions

This get-to-know-you activity swiftly demonstrates how much is assumed from first impressions and can lead on to more work around stereotyping.

Aim

For each participant to guess things about another member of the group based solely on what they look like.

You will need

- copies of the 'assumptions sheet' for each person
- pens.

How to do it

Hand out the assumption sheets and pens and invite each person to choose someone else in the group that they don't know very well to work with. No one needs to move, and the activity actually works better if they are seated across the room from each other; stress that they shouldn't communicate at all whilst they fill in the sheet.

Allow five to ten minutes for everyone to finish and then invite pairs in turn to feedback their 'assumptions'. Allow time to ask how conclusions were made on such limited information and sum up with a short discussion about the power of first impressions.

ASSUMPTIONS SHEET

Favourite food	
Favourite music	
Favourite clothes shop	
Favourite magazine	
Favourite book of all time	
Favourite hobby	
Favourite sport	
Favourite TV programme	
Favourite subject at school	
Perfect weekend	
Ideal holiday destination	

2.4   Hot seat

This is a group warm-up to help the young women get to know each other better. It works best if you use it to start a session after the young women have met a few times.

Aim

To use active listening skills and introduce the idea of non-verbal communication.

You will need

- nothing!

How to do it

As the group arrive ask each of them to think of three things about themselves that they would like to share with the group – then set the rule that two of these should be true but the third should be made up! Invite them to be as creative as possible, but remind them of your confidentiality boundaries if you think this may be an issue.

Now ask the group to make a circle and set a 'hot seat' into the circle. This should be where everyone can see. In turn invite each young woman to sit on the 'hot seat' and share her three things. For example:

'The first thing about me is that I support Arsenal, the second is that I have four brothers, the third is that I have eaten frog's legs on holiday in France!'

The rest of the group should be encouraged to listen carefully to what is being said and to watch for any changes in body language whilst the three things are being told. Offer a quick résumé of what has been said to remind the group and then ask who thinks number one, two or three are false using a show of hands. Review after each go – were they wrong or right? What gave it away when someone lied? How different did they look when giving truthful information? Discuss any surprises or unusual revelations!

2.5   Group crests

This is a group activity to get to know each other and build skills in representing others.

Aim

To produce a 'crest' that is representative of the whole group, showing individuals as well as shared interests.

You will need

- paper
- markers.

How to do it

As the young women come in ask them to take a seat at a table. Set a rule that they cannot move the chairs, so if the table is full they must find another seat. Each table should have about four to six seats around it.

Once everyone has a seat explain that the task is for each group to design a 'crest' that shows everyone on their table. It needs to represent characteristics of each individual as well as things that the young women have in common. The only rule is that everyone must be included in the discussion and take ownership of the final design.

Allow about 20 minutes for the artwork to be completed. It will take longer if you have a lot of groups. When they have finished, ask the young women to display their crests in the centre of the table.

Next allow 'gallery' time so that everyone can view all the crests. This is not a competition but an opportunity to share. In turn each group stands by their crest and answers any questions the rest of the young women may have.

Review the process. Does everyone feel that they are fully represented? How easy was it to negotiate things that represented everyone? How were individual attributes chosen?

2.6 Animal perceptions

Aim

This is a simple and thought-provoking activity that makes the point that others can see us differently from how we see ourselves.

You will need

- copies of the 'animal perceptions sheet'
- paper and pens.

How to do it

Start the activity with some discussion about how other people can affect the way that people see themselves. Ask the young women to suggest some celebrities and then go through how they are seen by the media/public and then reflect if this could be different from how they perceive themselves. One example could be high-profile Angelina Jolie: sex symbol or devoted mother? Can you be both?

Next, hand out paper and pens and ask the young women to rank the animals below in order of their personal preference with one being favourite and four being least favourite.

1. Lion
2. Dog
3. Parrot
4. Elephant

When everyone has written their list, hand out copies of the 'animal perceptions sheet'. Make sure you stress that this is just for fun, not a scientific psychometric assessment; the point is to encourage thinking about who we are and who we want to be.

Some discussion points:

- How do we shape our self-image according to the opinions of other people?
- Do we understand how others see us?
- To what extent does what other people think of us matter?
- Can you think of a person that has influenced the way you do/see things?

ANIMAL PERCEPTIONS SHEET

		Dog	Lion	Elephant	Parrot
1	How you want other people to see you	Friendly, loyal, faithful, supportive, protective, dependable, reliable, trustful, trusting, solid, hardworking, loving	Loud, in charge, can be bossy, independent, makes decisions, starts things, group leader, critical but fair, focused, brave	Tolerant, passive, co-operative, respected, big, strong, controlled, calm, can take the lead, listened to, wise	Lively, fun, free-spirited, sociable, good tempered, popular, attractive, cheerful, passionate, spontaneous
2	How you think others see you now				
3	How you'd like to be seen by others in the future				
4	How you actually want to be – without outside influence				

2.7   Against the rules!

This is an activity for medium-sized groups, although you could adapt it for individual work. It is intended to be fun, so encourage the young women to think as widely as possible!

Aim

This is a warm-up activity to provoke discussions before a more in-depth look at female stereotypes.

You will need

- nothing!

How to do it

Divide the young women into groups of three or four and specify different areas within the room for each group to work.

Now in their groups ask them to think about things that people might believe to be 'against the rules' for women to do. The idea is to gain an understanding of any views or beliefs that the young women may hold so encourage them by asking questions such as:

- Are there 'men's jobs' and 'women's jobs'?
- Is some behaviour acceptable for men but not women?

Once they have had a chance to discuss their thoughts, set each group the task of choosing one thing that is 'against the rules' and devising a short mime, role-play or song that acts it out. If you know that your group will just hate anything that involves drama adapt it and ask them to draw it or devise a short cartoon. Stress that whatever they choose it shouldn't actually mention what it is that they are showing!

Allow 15–20 minutes for the groups to get ready and then invite them to take it in turns to show their piece. After each group has presented, lead a round of applause and then ask the rest of the young women to guess what it is they are portraying.

When everyone has presented lead a discussion about where ideas have come from. Is it something they have heard other people saying? On the TV? Is it how women are portrayed in the magazines they read? Conclude by reflecting on how true or untrue these stereotypes are and use the information gained to develop further sessions.

2.8   Who am I?

This is a version of a popular game at parties and in schools, so you will usually find at least one member of the group who knows how to play it. If this is so, ask them to explain the rules to the others.

Aim

This is a warm-up activity to build confidence and a sense of achievement within the group.

You will need

- post-it notes with the names of famous women written on them.

How to do it

Explain that for this activity each young woman will be given the name of a famous woman that she will need to guess by asking questions to the rest of the group.

Ask for a volunteer player to go first.

Stick one of the post-it notes onto the volunteer's forehead, where they cannot see it but the rest of the group can. Show it to the group so that they can clearly see who it is, for example 'Charlotte Church' or 'Michelle Obama'.

Now, encourage the player to ask the group questions to help them work out who it is. Stress that the others can only give them 'yes' or 'no' answers. If the young woman finds this difficult or is struggling, start them off with some questions to base their own ideas on. For example 'Is this woman a singer?' rather than 'Is she an actress or a singer?'

The player can make a guess at any time. If they are correct then the person who answered the last question takes their place, a new name is given and the game begins again. If they are wrong then the player will need to ask more questions.

It is suggested that you set a time limit or agree the number of questions that can be asked during each round to keep the pace fast and ensure that there is time for every group member to take a turn.

2.9   The name game

This is a good icebreaker for young women of any age. You can change the focus to suit other themes.

Aim

To make positive personal statements and get to know each other's names.

You will need

- nothing!

How to do it

Ask the young women to form a circle facing each other.

Explain that what you want is for people to say their name and use a positive word to describe herself. Make sure that you stress that this attribute can be physical or emotional and that it is not up for debate by other members of the group. So for example Brigit may be Beautiful or Brainy – it is up to her!

There is a catch! It has to begin with the same letter as their name and no one can duplicate the adjectives no matter how many girls there are in the group with the same name!

If you think the group will be shy about this, start the process off yourself and encourage the young people to be as creative as they can. This is usually a fairly easy activity…unless, like me, your name is Vanessa, in which case your adjective options are limited!

Continue to the next person who should introduce herself and then the person sitting next to them. Keep going until everyone has had a turn.

2.10   Pass the face

This is a fun game that is a good warm-up to use before a session on non-verbal communication.

Aim

To build trust and encourage the young women to relax in the group – and it always gets a smile!

You will need

- nothing!

How to do it

The idea of this game is to pass a facial expression. The principles of it are the same as 'whispers', where a message is whispered from person to person but this version uses non-verbal communication.

Ask the young women to sit in a circle and ask for a volunteer. Have everyone close her eyes except the volunteer who is going to pass a 'face'.

The passer then taps the shoulder of the girl next to her who should open her eyes to receive the face. She then taps the shoulder of the person next to her and passes the face along, trying hard to keep it as close to what was shown as possible.

Keep going around the circle, explaining that once you have passed the face you can keep your eyes open to watch it move around the group! At the end, the original volunteer receives the face back from the last person in the group and then shows everyone what the original face was!

2.11   Active listening

You can make this activity as hard or as easy as you like, depending on the pictures you choose!

Aim

To demonstrate the need for active listening to be able to complete a task.

You will need

- one picture that is very simple, for example a photo of a classical building
- one picture that is complicated, for example an abstract photo of a building
- pencils
- sheets of plain paper.

How to do it

Make photocopies of each picture so that there are enough for each member of the group.

Ask the group to work in pairs and hand out pencils to everyone. Ask the young women to sit on chairs back to back so that they can't see each other's face.

Now, for each pair give a copy of the first picture to one young woman and a copy of the second picture to the other. Stress that they should not show each other what they have or it won't work!

Explain that in turn they are going to describe the picture they have been given to their partner, who will then draw what they hear. Each round will take five to ten minutes.

Once each young woman has had their turn at drawing and describing ask the group to stop, turn around and show their partner the picture that they were given. Spend time in pairs comparing what was drawn and what was on the actual picture. How close are they?

As a whole group review the process. What made it easy to listen? What instructions were hard to understand? Why? Make the point that it is easier to describe something you can see clearly and understand fully. Often it is harder to talk about concepts or ideas that you haven't thought about before and so put your own interpretation on.

2.12   Shared goals activity

This activity works best when the young women know each other well enough to share things about themselves, but not so well that they know everything!

Aim

The aim of this activity is to discover shared goals and also to identify core personal goals.

You will need

- copies of the 'goal cards' copied onto card and cut up and put into an envelope
- flipchart paper and markers.

How to do it

Divide the young people into pairs or groups of four maximum. Hand each group a pack of the cards, a marker and a sheet of flipchart paper.

Explain that the cards in the envelope represent different goals that people may have. Stress that everyone thinks differently and that no card has a higher value than another.

Now, ask them to draw a Venn diagram (two overlapping circles) on the flipchart sheet. Explain that each circle represents a group member and the intersection in the middle where the circles meet represents the whole group. Invite the young people to write their names alongside the circle that will be theirs.

Invite each group to look through their cards and discuss the goals on each. If they think that a card is one of their own personal core values then they should place it in the circle with their name on. If it is a value that is important to more than one, but not all, of the group then suggest they use the marker to write it in both participants' circles. If it is not a concern for anyone then it can be placed back into the envelope. If it is an important value for everyone in the group it can be placed into the middle section. Allow time for discussion and then ask the group to decide on three core values that they all hold.

Once everyone has completed the task, invite the young people to look at each other's Venn diagram. Encourage questions and discussions about the values that the whole group holds, as well as individuals. Review the activity and ask what they have learnt about each other. Ask how easy it is to uphold personal values if they are not shared within a group. Facilitate a discussion that looks at the issues around maintaining personal values and beliefs whilst accepting that others may not share them.

GOAL CARDS

Take better care of myself	Get organised
Strengthen my family	Get more involved in my community
Obtain housing	Get more involved in cultural or ethnic activities
Access health care	Find a job
Manage stress	Enhance / set up routines
Manage moods / emotions	Enhance family togetherness
Manage money better	Devote more time to my spiritual life
Manage anger	Deal with school-related issues

GOAL CARDS

Make better decisions	Continue my education / training
Reduce alcohol / drugs	Communicate better
Improve personal appearance	Choose friends and companions wisely
Improve social supports	Be more consistent
Improve relationships	Become more independent
Improve physical fitness	Improve financial situation
Improve personal hygiene	Improve my social life
Have more time for myself	Have a safe home

2.13   Values tree

This is shown as a small group activity, but it works just as well with individuals.

Aim

To discuss and share values and beliefs.

You will need

- flipchart and coloured markers.

How to do it

Divide the young women into groups of three to five and give each group a sheet of paper and a good selection of markers.

Set each group the task of drawing a tree on their sheet. The tree must include a root system, trunk, branches, leaves, fruit and flowers. Once they have done this ask each group to think about their tree in terms of the 'tree key'. They will need to discuss and agree things to write in each part of the tree so that it is reflective of all of them.

Write up the 'tree key' so that all participants can see it.

Invite each group to introduce their tree, making reference to the members and which bits represent them. Encourage questions and discussion and then display all the trees.

Tree key

Roots = family/cultural influences and beliefs

Trunk = personal values and beliefs

Branches = important relationships

Leaves = skills

Fruit = ideas and hopes for the future

Flowers = achievements and strengths

2.14   Bumper stickers

This activity increases self-esteem and encourages young women to share personal information.

Aim

For the young women to express themselves in a positive way.

You will need

- a large sheet of paper or card
- Blu-Tack
- sheets of paper (cut into three strips)
- glue
- markers
- glitter.

How to do it

In preparation for the session, draw the back view of a car onto a large sheet of paper. This needs to be big enough to display everyone's bumper sticker.

Begin the session by suggesting that a bumper sticker is chosen to represent something about the owner of the car it's stuck on. This could include places the person has visited, their values, jokes, political opinions, musical preferences, etc. Invite the young women to share the best or worst ones that they have seen.

Next, set the young women the task of designing their own bumper stickers and hand out the strips of paper. Make a good selection of markers, glitter and glue available. Stress that the sticker they design should say something about themselves, their likes or beliefs.

Once the group has finished working on their individual stickers, introduce the car picture and stick it up on a wall where everyone can see it. Then in turn invite each young woman to take the glue and stick her bumper sticker on the car. As they do it ask them to explain why they put particular messages, etc. on their 'stickers', and encourage questions from the rest of the group.

Chapter 3

Self-Esteem and Body Image

3.1   Music, lines and emotions

Aim

This activity encourages young women to explore the concept of expressing their emotions through music and art.

You will need

- a selection of music
- permanent markers
- paint brushes
- paint
- paper plates
- water
- A3 paper (approx 11 x 17").

How to do it

To prepare for the session, make a playlist of clips of music. Try to include tracks from different genres, for example Spanish flamenco, ambient chill, thrash metal and West African drumming and percussion music. Make sure it is not something instantly recognisable, as familiarity will give different results. Set up tables with A3 paper on, markers and the painting equipment.

Start the session by suggesting that music can influence or express mood. Invite examples from the young women, for example music you might play whilst getting ready to go out or songs that mean a lot.

Now explain that you want each young woman to take a sheet of paper and a marker pen. They should then close their eyes and draw lines with the marker to reflect the emotions they think are conveyed by each track that you play. These can be as simple or as complex as they feel appropriate.

After each piece played, stop and ask the young women to reflect and share what they have drawn. Once all the tracks have been played, ask participants to select the drawing they feel is the most powerful. Make the painting equipment available and ask the group to now choose colour to represent the emotions of the music.

Allow 20 minutes for everyone to work on their painting and then facilitate a gallery time inviting each person to introduce their work by explaining which genre of music inspired the drawing, what it made them feel and how they have expressed these feelings.

Finally suggest that this method is a really good way of expressing emotions and that they might like to try it outside of the group, for example as a way of expressing stress or feelings of anger.

3.2   Personal poems

This activity can be done individually or in pairs. It is similar to the fridge magnet kits you can buy where you are given an assortment of words to make up rhymes or poems from, so some young women will be familiar with the concept.

Aim

For young women to use key words as the basis of a poem about themselves.

You will need

- post-it notes
- pens
- 'word cards' copied onto card and cut up (one set each pair)
- magazines
- A4 paper (approx 8.5 x 11")
- example poems or song words (optional).

How to do it

Introduce the activity and share any examples you have.

In pairs (or individually) ask the women to idea-storm key words that they think describe themselves to other people. Encourage their partner to add positive suggestions too. This can include how they look, what they like or beliefs they hold – anything that they think is really important. They should write these onto post-it notes as they go along.

Next ask the young women to individually choose words, lines of text or slogans and put them with their key words to make a short poem. Make sure you stress that there are lots of different kinds of poetry and that it doesn't have to rhyme. Once they are happy with their poem, ask them to write it up onto the A4 paper, decorating the page with pictures or symbols either drawn or cut from magazines.

Display and arrange gallery time so that everyone in the group can share their work.

WORD CARDS

is	with	change	happy	if
are	more	care	at	I
say	as	go	true	do
his	hers	she	he	special
here	by	always	and	family
had	tell	like	to	too
dream	remember	ask	time	every
for	you	in	it	go
there	from	thoughts	together	good
after	grow	were	can	are
why	me	how	you	laugh
past	history	meaning	love	save
happy	sad	thinking	back	future
heritage	teach	hold	love	said
home	use	this	life	still

put	dirt	slice	left	right
young	old	mother	father	grandmother
grandfather	have	little	big	ways
our	photo	day	night	people
leave	when	went	will	want
always	me	mine	myself	over
live	before	please	thanks	sister
brother	off	friendship	friend	never
forever	only	has	my	no
faith	hope	not	book	music
words	spirit	truth	full	stop
away	towards	sky	earth	tomorrow
give	gave	about	family	teach
yes	man	woman	build	like
the	only	lonely	out	a

3.3   Chain reaction

Aim

This exercise encourages participants to share the things they are good at and appreciate the talents of other members of the group.

You will need

- packets of unmade paper chains
- marker pens.

How to do it

Begin by asking the young women, 'What do you think that you do well?' Stress that this doesn't have to be an academic achievement but can be anything. After a brief discussion, conclude that everyone is talented in some way.

Now, hand out five of the unmade paper chains to each member of the group. Using markers, ask everyone to write one talent on each strip of paper.

Demonstrate how to make a paper chain, using the five strips and linking them together. As the young women begin to complete their mini chains, use extra strips of paper to link the mini chains together to create one long group chain. Invite the young women to stand and hold the ever-growing chain as you link it together, until everyone is linked.

Once the entire chain is constructed and linked together, hang the chain up in the room as a reminder that everyone is good at something. Encourage the group to look at the different talents and skills within the group and refer to these during future group sessions.

3.4   Advertising me

When you collect together magazines for this task make sure you gather a wide range, including publications aimed at young men and LGBT (lesbian, gay, bisexual and transgender) youth.

Aim

To promote increased self-esteem and to identify positive personality traits.

You will need

- magazines
- scissors
- glue
- flipchart paper
- markers.

How to do it

Introduce the young women to advertisements cut out of the magazines. Talk about their purpose and the method by which ads get the message across – visually and with words. Explain that ads promote the positive aspects of a product, the finer qualities. Remind the girls that the prime objective of an advert is to persuade a person into buying the product.

Now go on to say that the young women's task in this project is to come up with an advertisement persuading someone to be their friend. Each young woman should depict positive aspects of themselves through pictures, words, or a combination of the two. Hand out a good selection of markers, glue, scissors and magazines plus a sheet of flipchart paper each.

If anyone has a difficult time thinking of reasons someone would want to be their friend, have them think of characteristics that they look for in a friend. At the end of the session invite the young women to share advertisements with one another. Encourage other members of the group to confirm the positive qualities of the presenter.

Finally display the adverts so that the whole group can see them.

3.5   What is beauty?

If you have a small group play this as a sorting game, placing all the cards in the middle and asking the young women to place them in order of historical date.

Aim

To explore the changing 'ideal' body shape of women through the decades.

You will need

- pictures of women in underwear through the decades from the stays and corsets of the early twentieth century through to today's bras.

You can find good examples of these online: 'Underwear through the ages' from the *Daily Mail* (www.dailymail.co.uk/femail/article-1191774) and the Fashion and Textile Museum (www.ftm/london.org).

How to do it

To prepare for the session go online to the suggested websites (and any others you can find) and print off pictures of underwear models. Make sure you encompass changing trends, including examples from the 1920s where the fashion was to 'flatten' breasts through to the 'push it up' hourglass figures of Hollywood starlets of the 1940s and 1950s. You will immediately see how the shape of women has changed radically down the years, with the most contemporary pictures featuring very thin models.

Shuffle the pictures (mount them onto card if you are planning to use the resource more than once), and then hand them to the young women. Their task is to, one by one, show the rest of the group their picture and then place it in a continuum, placing the picture that they think is the oldest at one end and the most recent at the other. Make a rule that no one else can chip in or move the picture until all the cards have been put down.

Once you have all the cards laid, stop and review the process as a whole group. Invite comments and allow cards to be moved around until everyone is happy that the continuum is right. Then tell the group the right order.

Now, facilitate a discussion that considers the following:

1. Has the concept of the 'ideal' size for an underwear model changed?

2. Which era featured models that reflect 'real' women?

3. Does what is shown affect the way that women think? Or feel?

Conclude by summing up the changes from the earlier concept of beauty being curvy women, through to modern adverts, which tend to feature women who are very slender but who have large breasts. Point out that the average dress size for women in the UK is a 16 (US 14), with the average female measurements being a bust of 38.5 inches (98 cm), a waist of 34 inches (86 cm) and hips of 40.5 inches (103 cm) and size 6 feet. In the US, the average clothing size is not a size 8 for women; it is a 14, the size at which 'plus-sized' clothing begins (the same as the UK). How does this compare with the women modelling? For more information on this and related topics go to www.campaignforrealbeauty.co.uk.

3.6   Body image

This is a small-group follow-on from the previous activity, although it can be used on its own. You need to have been working with the group for some time so that they feel comfortable participating.

Aim

To create discussions around body image.

You will need

- flipchart paper stuck together or a large roll of paper
- post-it notes in two different colours
- markers.

How to do it

Before you start this activity ensure that you have a group contract agreed with the young women, which includes agreements about confidentiality and respect to promote a safe and inclusive environment. Then ask for a volunteer and carefully draw around her to create a life size body silhouette.

Next hand out post-it notes to the young women and ask them to write statements on them about things they don't like about their appearances. For example, 'I don't like my eyes' or 'I don't like my thighs' etc.

Each young woman should then take a turn in placing her post-it notes onto the 'body' in the corresponding place. After each go, stop and invite the rest of the group to write positive points about that person on the other coloured post-it notes and then stick them onto the body.

Reflect on the differences – how easy is it to see positives in yourself? Are there some attributes that are seen as negatives by the person who has them, but seen as positive attributes by her peers? For example, Amy may think that she is too tall, but other members of the group may see her height as a real attribute.

You can then go on to talk about where ideals of womanhood and beauty come from. For example fashion models and celebrities with size zero bodies or surgically enhanced breasts shown in magazines. What is the 'perfect body'? Reinforce the need for healthy eating and explore this in further sessions.

3.7   What makes a woman?

This is explained as a group activity for six to eight young women, but you could adapt it for individual use too.

Aim

To encourage the young women to think about what physical, emotional and mental attributes make a 'woman'.

You will need

- a roll of white wallpaper or lining paper cut and stuck together so that it is big enough for a life size human shape to be drawn on it (alternatively stick pieces of flipchart paper together)
- markers.

How to do it

Briefly explain the session and then ask for a volunteer. Unroll the stuck-together wallpaper and invite the volunteer to lie down on it, so that there is paper all around her.

Next ask for a volunteer to draw around her, making sure that you refer to any group contract and the need to respect personal space. Once it is done ask both volunteers to return to the main group and place marker pens on the silhouette.

Now encourage the young women to think about what 'makes a woman' in their view.

Inside the body they should write physical factors, for example breasts, a vagina or the ability to have a baby, and emotional attributes that in their opinion are feminine.

Outside the body, the young women should write words that describe what they believe society/boys/family think makes a woman. For example having long hair or big breasts, polite manners, a gentle caring attitude, non-aggressive behaviour and the skills to be a good homemaker.

Once the 'woman' is complete, review what has been written. How are our views of 'what makes a woman' affected? Include the impact of mothers or other significant females, religion and culture as well as outside influences such as the TV, advertising and magazines. Who decides?

3.8   Self-esteem – what is it?

Aim

This is an introductory exercise to discuss the meaning of self-esteem.

You will need

- copies of the 'self-esteem cards'.

How to do it

Divide the young women into small group of three or four. Give each group a set of the self-esteem cards.

Their task is to discuss each card and then rank it in terms of importance, putting the statements they think best describe self-esteem at the top, and the ones they think are least relevant and important last.

Allow about 15 minutes for discussion and then ask if each group has reached consensus. Next, facilitate a feedback session inviting each group to share their top selections and the reasons why these were chosen. Encourage discussion and ask the young women to reflect on why having good self-esteem is important.

Finally, hand each young woman a post-it note and pen and ask them to individually rank their own self-esteem between one and five, with one meaning low and five meaning high.

If this activity is part of a wider self-esteem programme, collect in the post-it notes and keep. Repeat the exercise at the end of the final session so that the young women can compare their self-scores and reflect on progress.

If it is a one-off session, encourage the young women to share their personal assessment and agree one personal target to increase self-esteem.

SELF-ESTEEM CARDS

Having personal goals and aspirations	Believing that I deserve love and respect	Feeling secure in myself
Being able to say what I do and don't want	Feeling worthy of my own happiness	Feeling that I can cope with life's pressures and stresses
Believing I deserve to be treated well by others	Liking myself	Feeling in control of my life and my choices
A positive belief in my own value	Taking the best possible care of myself	Knowing I have rights and responsibilities
Knowing that I can cope with changes in my life	Knowing myself and my capabilities	Feeling secure in my friendships
Believing that I have the right to express my feelings	Having the right to ask for help	Understanding that I will make mistakes

3.9   Self-esteem – Aimee's story

Aim

This is an exercise to encourage young women to think about the things that impact on self-esteem.

You will need

- A4 size photocopies of a picture of a young woman
- flipchart markers and pens.

How to do it

In advance choose a picture of a young woman and name her for the purpose of the exercise. This can be any female, but it should not be anybody recognisable to the group.

Hand each participant a copy and explain that you are going to tell a story about the young woman in the picture. Every time they hear something negative said about her, or something happens that could be upsetting, they should rip a piece off.

Tell the story:

> Aimee is 15 and her parents have just been through a very difficult divorce. Aimee moved with her mum miles away from their old house, which means that she doesn't get to see her dad or her best mate anymore.
>
> It is Monday morning and Aimee woke up late, so she is rushing to get ready for school.
>
> 'Are you out of that shower yet?' Aimee's mum shouts. 'You're going to be late!' To make her point she bangs loudly on the door and then continues, 'I can't imagine what you do in there that takes so long – it certainly doesn't show! Most of the time you look a right mess. Come on! Hurry up!'
>
> Aimee finishes in the bathroom and quickly darts back to the bedroom that she shares with her little sister.
>
> 'Have you tidied your room?' Aimee's mum shouts up the stairs. 'I told you to do it last night, but as usual you just ignored me and sat chatting to that silly friend of yours on the internet!'

'Err, yes, I think I did…' Aimee replies, knowing that she didn't. It doesn't seem fair, her sister is never asked to help and in their old house she had her own bedroom.

'What is the matter with you?' her mum shouts angrily. 'All I ask is for you to take a bit of responsibility for a change! It's not as if you ever do anything useful; you just mope about the house moaning! Why don't you go out and make new friends?'

Aimee hesitates; so much has changed recently and she doesn't seem to fit into any of the groups at school. She feels bad for her mum who is still really upset about her dad leaving them, but she is not happy either. 'I'm sorry!' she slowly says.

'Well, sorry isn't good enough, is it?' her mum yells. 'You know what? You are just like your useless father – perhaps you should go and live with him! Oh no, I forgot, he doesn't want you either!'

Aimee walks out of the house angry and upset; why can't her mum ever listen? Secretly Aimee wishes she could go and live with her dad, but she isn't sure that this is really an option as she has hinted several times to him, but he has ignored it. Perhaps no one wants me, she thinks.

As you finish, ask the young women to hold up what is left of their photo and suggest that what they are looking at is what is left of Aimee's self-esteem.

Divide the group into threes and ask them to discuss the story they have just heard.

1. What factors have impacted on Aimee's self-esteem?

2. What things can't be changed, for example the divorce?

3. What could be done to raise Aimee's self-esteem to enable her to cope better?

Bring the whole group back together and pull out and record the main points from each group.

3.10   Self-esteem mirror

Aim

An important first step in building self-esteem, this activity enables young women to take a realistic look at their strengths and weaknesses, likes and dislikes.

You will need

- paper and pens.

How to do it

Hand out a pen and paper to each girl and ask them to fold the paper in half lengthwise. Explain that this is now a mirror that will reflect back things about its owner. On one side of the mirror, they should list all the things they like about themselves. On the other side of the mirror, all the things they do not like. Ask the young women to compare the two lists. Which side has more on? Which was the more difficult to list?

Suggest that people with high self-esteem are realistic about their strengths and weaknesses and feel optimistic about setting achievable goals. They also feel good about themselves and do not take other people's negative impressions of them too seriously.

People with low self-esteem have a harder time honestly evaluating their strengths and weaknesses. This can lead to an overall negative impression of themselves that makes it easy to take other people's opinions more seriously than they should. Feeling bad about themselves can lead to people thinking that everything they do will fail before they even try.

Ask the young women to choose a partner to work with that they are happy to share their mirrors with. Allow time for each pair to look at their personal mirrors and encourage positive additions.

3.11   What shall I wear today?

This activity is based on the old game of paper dolls that you dress up with cut-out outfits. Because most young women will have heard of, or played, the game before it doesn't need much explaining!

Aim

To open discussions around appropriate clothing and how what we wear can influence people's perceptions of us.

You will need

- sets of 'occasions cards'
- large envelopes
- scissors
- card
- magazines
- clear sticky back plastic (optional).

How to do it

To prepare for the session look through a good selection of magazines and cut out as many different types of outfits as you can find, including those worn by stars. Cut out pictures of shoes and accessories too! Make sure you have everything from nightwear to dresses worn by stars to attend premières, glamour girl outfits, daywear and sports clothes. You will need enough to provide at least 20 choices for each group of four young women. When you have collected together the pictures, you can cover them in clear sticky back plastic to make them easier to reuse and less likely to get damaged. Then place each selection into a large envelope.

Next enlarge and photocopy the 'occasions cards'. Once again you are going to need enough so that each group of four has a set to work with.

When the young women arrive divide them into groups of four or five. Explain that the task you are setting them is to look into the envelope and agree outfits to wear to the occasions shown on the cards. The only ground rule is that they all have to agree which clothes they would wear and be ready to share why.

Allow at least 30 minutes for discussion and then ask each group to lay their cards out onto the floor with the outfit of choice placed on top.

Now facilitate a feedback session asking each group in turn what they have chosen for an event and why they think that their choices are appropriate. Encourage groups to question each other.

Develop this into a discussion asking the young women to consider issues such as first impressions, stereotypes and finally keeping safe. For example, if you are going clubbing but know that you have to get home on public transport late at night should this affect your choice of clothing?

OCCASIONS CARDS

First date	Meeting partner's parents for the first time
Job interview	Night in with the girls
Clubbing	Youth club
Relative's wedding	The gym
Day out shopping with friends	Picnic in the park
Watching a band	Non-uniform day at school
A film première	Birthday dinner with parents
Sleepover with friends	Visit to relatives

3.12   Who is confident?

Aim

This group activity uses well-known celebrities as a discussion prompt and asks young women to assess their own levels of confidence.

You will need

- pictures of celebrities cut out of magazines
- flipchart and marker
- Blu-Tack.

How to do it

Divide the main group into small groups and hand each a selection of pictures of celebrities. Each group should discuss their pictures considering the following questions:

1. Which celebrities are confident?
2. How do they show they are confident?
3. Which aren't? How do they behave?

Draw a continuum on a sheet of flipchart marked 'Confident' at one end and 'Not Confident' at the other.

Now, in rotation invite each group to choose a celebrity and share the conclusions reached before sticking them onto the continuum where they think they should go. Encourage discussion as each celebrity is placed onto the board. Finally, invite each young woman to place themselves between the 'Confident' and 'Not Confident' poles.

3.13   Feelings scale

Emotional literacy is the ability to understand your own emotions, and those of others, and develop the ability to express feelings effectively.

Aim

This activity encourages young women to develop their vocabulary of feelings and explore different ways to express themselves.

You will need

- flipchart paper
- pens
- 'feelings sheets' listing six key emotions.

How to do it

Before the group arrives make up 'feelings sheets' by taking six flipchart paper sheets and individually heading them 'Anger', 'Happiness', 'Fear', 'Disgust' 'Surprise' and 'Sadness'

Divide the young women into six groups. Hand each group one of the feelings sheets and explain that each one will have a different key emotion written on the top. Ask them to collectively write down as many words as they can think of associated with that key emotion, for example anger, irritation, annoyance, fury, rage, aggression, violence, hate.

Allow ten minutes for this. Now ask the young women to rank each word according to intensity, for example ecstasy, joy, pleasure, amusement.

Once they have agreed a 'feelings scale' invite each group to share their work. Encourage comments from the rest of the larger group – is everybody in agreement with the rankings?

Finally ask the young women to form pairs. Taking it in turns, each partner should talk for three minutes about something important to them. This can be past, present, or future, using as many feelings words as possible. If you think that this may not be comfortable for everyone choose positive experiences to share or reduce the time to one minute each.

3.14   That makes me stressed!

Aim

To identify personal triggers and develop strategies to reduce stress.

You will need

- copies of the 'that makes me stressed!' sheet
- pens.

How to do it

Start by suggesting that everyone feels stressed at some point and that it is useful to be able to identify personal triggers in order to think about strategies to reduce it.

Explain that the sheet you are handing out is intended as a starting point for identifying sources of stress. Ask the young women to read through quietly and place a tick by any of the suggestions that stress them out. If they have a personal source of stress that is not mentioned they can write it on the bottom.

Once everyone has finished, ask the girls to turn to their left and share one or two examples from their sheets, considering:

1. What emotions does this stress provoke?

2. How do you cope with your feelings?

Bring the whole group back together and take some feedback, particularly drawing attention to similarities and coping strategies. Now as a whole group consider positive strategies to handle stress and record these once agreement is reached.

After the session get these ideas typed up and made into small 'stress strategy sheets' to give out the following week. You could also add details of any local youth support services that could help.

THAT MAKES ME STRESSED!

Emotional well-being means having the inner strength, resilience and self-esteem to cope with life's problems and make the most of life's opportunities. However, we all have times when we find it harder to cope.

Have a look through the following and place a tick beside those that you consider personal stress or anxiety triggers:

- ☐ Someone I care about being ill
- ☐ Feeling disrespected
- ☐ Going to a social event where I don't know many people
- ☐ Gaining a new family member
- ☐ Someone getting angry with me in public
- ☐ Having too much work to do
- ☐ A friend letting me down by betraying a secret
- ☐ Preparing for an exam or interview
- ☐ Arguing with someone I care about
- ☐ Moving home
- ☐ Being unwell
- ☐ Being asked to do something I don't want to do
- ☐ Not getting enough sleep
- ☐ Starting a new school/college/job
- ☐ People not doing what they say they will
- ☐ Being made late for something important
- ☐ Someone challenging my values or beliefs
- ☐ Getting into debt
- ☐ Someone telling lies about me
- ☐ Giving up a bad habit
- ☐ Feeling guilty about something I did
- ☐ Seeing an ex-partner for the first time after splitting up

3.15   Assertiveness quiz

Most young women are familiar with quizzes such as this in magazines so will need minimum support to engage with this activity.

Aim

To look at the differences between being 'assertive', 'passive' and 'aggressive' and provoke discussion within the group.

You will need

- copies of the 'assertiveness quiz'
- pens.

How to do it

Hand out a pen and a copy of the quiz to each young woman. Explain that you want them to work on their own to begin with, but if you know that some group members will struggle with this suggest pairs.

Introduce the quiz by saying that there is a series of situations and possible responses shown on the page. You want the girls to look and tick the response that they feel would be closest to their own reaction in a similar circumstance.

Once everyone has finished ask the group to come together. Read out the questions and the answers and ask the young women to keep a tally of how many 'a', 'b' and 'c's they have ticked as you go through the sheet.

Finally ask the girls to count and see which letter they have ticked the most and read aloud the corresponding paragraphs below. Stress that no one needs to share scores, but do encourage feedback. Do they agree with the quiz? How easy is it to say what you want? What is the difference between being assertive and being aggressive? How can you be more assertive without becoming aggressive?

Mainly a

You don't always need to go along with everyone else! There is nothing wrong with being you and making your feelings and opinions known. You need to look at ways to give clearer messages that reflect what you really want.

MAINLY B

You are comfortable with being assertive, whilst remaining sensitive to other people's needs. You expect people to respect who you are and offer respect back. Make sure that you maintain this even when things get difficult!

MAINLY C

Steady there! You will find that people are more ready to listen to you if you give them space and look at other ways to get your message across rather than getting angry and loud. You may be right but no one will listen if you don't calm down!

ASSERTIVENESS QUIZ

Look at the situations and responses below. Some are 'aggressive', some are 'passive' and some are 'assertive'. Which one sounds most like you?

1. You are accused by your teacher of something you didn't do in front of the class. Do you:

   (a) Say nothing and avoid speaking to the teacher again.

   (b) Say nothing at the time, but stay behind after class and explain that you didn't do it.

   (c) Shout 'It wasn't me!' then walk out – no one talks to you like that.

2. You are in a café and the burger and chips you order is served cold. Do you:

   (a) Just cover it in ketchup and eat what you can – you feel embarrassed to say something and it is very busy in the café.

   (b) Ask the waiter to come over and calmly explain that the food is cold and that you would like him to replace it.

   (c) Shout at the waiter and demand to see the manager – how dare they serve you cold food?

3. You go to your doctor with a health concern, but you don't really understand what she tells you. Do you:

   (a) Say thank you and leave – you can always check it on the internet at home.

   (b) Be assertive and ask her if she can explain again as you didn't understand it all.

   (c) Tell her that the visit has been a total waste of your time, as you didn't understand a word.

4. You go to the family planning clinic to get some free condoms. When you get there the person you usually see isn't there. Do you:

   (a) Go home – you will just have to take a chance until the person you know is there.

   (b) Take a deep breath and tell the new person what you want.

(c)   March over and demand the condoms – you know your rights.

5.   Someone you really fancy compliments you on your appearance at a party. Do you:

(a)   Blush, look at the floor and then walk off.

(b)   Smile, make eye contact and say thank you.

(c)   Move in close, wink and tell them they look pretty good too!

6.   You are standing in a queue for the bus and someone pushes in front of you. Do you:

(a)   Say nothing – they may have a go at you.

(b)   Tap them on the shoulder politely and explain that there is a queue.

(c)   Shove past when the bus arrives and stare hard at them if they look like saying something.

7.   Your best mate keeps borrowing money and not giving it back. She wants to borrow another £10. Do you:

(a)   Lend it to her – it is only money and she may not want to be your friend anymore if you say no.

(b)   Tell her firmly that although she is your friend you cannot lend her any more money.

(c)   Tell her the bank is shut! No way!

8.   You get home to discover that your sister has found and read your diary. Do you:

(a)   Tell your mum – she can deal with it.

(b)   Tell her how angry you are – your diary is private and you feel that she has shown you no respect by going through your things.

(c)   Scream, shout and threaten her with physical violence – she deserves it!

3.16   This is my life

Life story work can bring up all sorts of issues so you need to put very tight boundaries around it and assess whether it is appropriate for your group.

Aim

To look at key women in the young women's past and the impact they have on their present life.

You will need

- a photo of each young woman
- large sheets of paper
- markers/pens
- glue
- glitter, sequins, material, etc. (optional).

How to do it

Start by saying that we all have a life history, made up of events, memories and dreams, but the stories and family history that we are told by other women in our family, mothers, grandmothers and carers, also contribute to who we are and how we see the world around us. Explain that this activity makes the connection between past, present and future and enables young women to explore their heritage.

Ask the young women to turn the paper so that it is landscape and then draw a 'river' across the centre of the page from one side to the other. Once this is done suggest that this is now the 'river of life'. Ask the young women to stick their photo onto the right hand side of the paper at the end of the river and explain that this represents the present, the here and now.

Now ask them to think about women family members/carers who are important to them, or that they know about, going back as many generations as they can. Make sure that you say that information will be shared later to give everyone the option of censoring things.

When they are ready, invite the young women to put their key figures onto the river of life, stretching back into the past. Stress that this is not a drawing exercise, so they can represent people as they choose. Encourage them to write, or draw symbols or pictures to explain a bit about the women they have chosen, for example where they lived, what work they did or any stories that they know about them.

Allow about 30 minutes for the rivers to be completed and then invite the group to make a circle and share information. Facilitate a discussion afterwards asking the group to think about these questions:

- What is different about their lives compared to that of their ancestors?

- What traditions or rituals continue?

- What questions would they like to ask them if they could?

- What links can they see between the past, 'heritage' and their own lives?

3.17   Horoscopes

This is an activity for small group work and can be adapted to use with young women who do not enjoy reading and writing tasks by substituting pictures for words.

Aim

To encourage the young women to look ahead and start to set goals.

You will need

- magazine/newspaper horoscopes for that day or week
- 'my horoscope' sheets and pens.

How to do it

Seat the young women in a circle and open the session by sharing the horoscopes from the newspaper or magazine you have selected. Facilitate a short discussion around horoscopes, how true they are likely to be, why people read them, etc.

Hand out the 'my horoscope' sheets and pens and explain that you are now going to 'fast-forward' each young woman to age 25. Ask them to write their own horoscope for their life now at 25.

Explain that they should include hopes, dreams and ambitions and how they feel about themselves and also how others will see them if they achieve these.

Once everyone has a horoscope invite them back to the circle to share. Encourage questions and pull out positive points after each young woman finishes.

Following this, facilitate a discussion about hopes and dreams and how to achieve them, stressing the need for achievable goals. Introduce the idea of breaking targets down so that there are smaller goals that maximise incentive as they are reached. Close by agreeing one target each.

MY HOROSCOPE

These are the Zodiac signs and date ranges used in astrology. See which one is yours and then imagine yourself fast-forwarded to age 25. Devise a horoscope to show your hopes and aspirations.

Sign	Symbol	Dates
Aries	Ram	March 21 – April 19
Taurus	Bull	April 20 – May 20
Gemini	Twins	May 21 – June 20
Cancer	Crab	June 21 – July 22
Leo	Lion	July 23 – August 22
Virgo	Virgin	August 23 – September 22
Libra	Balance	September 23 – October 22
Scorpio	Scorpion	October 23 – November 21
Sagittarius	Archer	November 22 – December 21
Capricorn	Goat	December 22 – January 19
Aquarius	Water Bearer	January 20 – February 18
Pisces	Fish	February 19 – March 20

✔

Relationships ....

....

....

....

Family ....

....

....

....

Career ....

....

....

....

Lifestyle ....

....

....

....

Money ....

....

....

....

Housing ....

....

....

....

Chapter 4

Healthy Lifestyles

4.1   Stress gallery

Aim

This activity encourages young women to consider stress factors and develop some positive coping strategies.

You will need

- five large sheets of coloured paper
- a selection of coloured markers
- sticky tape
- flipchart paper.

How to do it

Ask the young women for a definition of stress. Emphasise that stress can cause powerful feelings, as well as biological changes in the body. Facilitate a short idea storm that suggests some of the feelings and biological changes that stress can cause.

Next, stick up five large sheets of coloured paper at different points in the room. Each sheet should have one of the headings below:

- Situations That Anger Me
- Situations That Worry Me
- Situations That Make Me Happy
- Situations That Make Me Excited
- Situations That Scare Me.

If you are working with a small group facilitate as a whole group activity, if not divide the main group into five smaller ones. Position each group next to one of the posters and hand out a selection of markers.

Each group has one to two minutes to write down their responses to the situation on the poster in front of them. When the designated time is up, ask each group to move to the poster on their right. Continue rotating until each group has had a chance to write their responses to the situations on all five posters.

Invite a spokesperson from each group to read the responses on the poster in front of them. Discuss similarities, insights, or perceptions related to the ideas listed. Talk about which responses are positive stressors and which are negative stressors. Conclude that stress isn't necessarily a bad thing; it can be positive in some situations.

As a group, consider healthy strategies to cope with the stressful situations identified, for example, going for a walk, playing sport, using art to express feelings or talking to someone. Record these on the flipchart paper and display or type up and distribute later.

4.2   Smoking and the media

Aim

This activity considers the ways in which smoking is portrayed in soap operas and the messages given.

You will need

- pictures of female soap stars
- access to the internet
- flipchart and markers.

How to do it

Collect pictures of well-known female soap characters, both smokers and non-smokers. The easiest place to get these is the official website for each programme.

Hand the young women the pile of pictures and ask them if they know which characters smoke and which ones don't. Facilitate a discussion that looks at the following:

1. Describe the female characters that smoke tobacco in Soap Land. Would this character be the same if she didn't? Why? Why not?

2. What about the women who don't smoke? Are they shown differently?

3. What messages about tobacco do you think this gives?

Encourage the young women to consider age, health, popularity and social status of the smokers.

Invite each group to share their conclusions, exploring any messages received, for example characters smoking when they are stressed or upset to feel better. Point out that Hollyoaks and High School Musical have no smoking policies that are strictly enforced, so that no characters smoke. Had they noticed this? Encourage the young women to consider what messages this gives.

Facilitate a show of hands to see who thinks that smoking should continue to be shown in soap operas, asking the young women to take into consideration facts such as the time that most soaps are shown as well as health issues. Display the photos along with the results of your poll.

4.3   Attitudes to alcohol

This activity is a good introductory session to work around alcohol issues.

Aim

To open up discussions about attitudes to drinking and to explore stereotypes.

You will need

- 'alcohol acceptable/unacceptable' sheets
- pens.

How to do it

Explain to the young women that you are going to hand each of them a sheet with a selection of alcohol-related statements on them. Some of these may be familiar, but stress that at this stage you are not asking if they have drunk alcohol before or engaged in any of the activities mentioned.

They should read through the statements and then place a tick in the box that reflects their opinion. Once everyone has completed their sheet go through it, stopping to encourage questions or to facilitate discussions where there is disagreement.

DISCUSSION POINTS

- Pull out some of the more emotive names for people who drink such as 'alcoholics' or 'drink drivers'. How do the media portray them? What do you think of when you hear these terms being used?

- Is it ever acceptable to blame bad behaviour on alcohol? Explore concepts of responsibility.

- Are women drinkers seen as less acceptable than men? Consider gender issues and reinforce that women are generally affected by alcohol faster than men. This is partly due to the fact that women are usually lighter and smaller than men but the main reason is that women have a higher fat to water ratio than men.

ALCOHOL ACCEPTABLE/UNACCEPTABLE

	Acceptable	Unacceptable
Drinking to get drunk on a night out		
Under-age drinking at house parties		
Drinking alcohol to celebrate		
Drinking alcohol if you are driving		
Using alcohol to help you relax if you feel stressed		
Drinking next day to cure a hangover		
Drinking on your own		
Having a drink before you go out to boost your confidence		
Accepting drinks from people you don't really know		
Not drinking alcohol at all		
Drinking alcohol with a family meal		
Drinking before or after a sporting fixture		
Buying alcohol as a Christmas or birthday present		
Using alcohol as an excuse when you have done something you regret		

4.4   What happens next?

This is shown as a small group activity but if you have a very small group give each young woman a scenario to work with.

Aim

To encourage young women to think through possible consequences of alcohol-related situations.

You will need

- a 'what happens next?' storyboard sheet for each group
- pens.

How to do it

Divide the large group into smaller groups of three or four. Hand each group a different scenario explaining that each depicts a situation where alcohol is an issue.

Using the storyboard sheet ask the young women to construct a comic strip to show what happens next. Encourage the groups to think about the consequences of actions, what they may have done differently in the situation and what could be done to resolve the scenario.

SCENARIOS

1. A 15-year-old young woman is caught at school drunk and with a can of extra-strength lager in her bag.

2. A 21-year-old young man buys a vodka-based alcopop for a 16-year-old young woman he has just met in a pub.

3. A 13-year-old young woman encourages an 18-year-old to buy alcohol for her from the shop/liquor store.

4. A 14-year-old young woman is drinking bottles of cider with friends at the park.

WHAT HAPPENS NEXT?

Use the storyboard to show what happens next...

4.5   A big night out

Aim

This activity encourages young women to take responsibility for personal safety and consider the potential risks involved in a 'big night out'.

You will need

- a set of 'big night out cards'
- three sheets of flipchart paper stuck together
- red, orange and green markers.

How to do it

In advance of the session use the flipchart paper stuck together to make a set of traffic lights by drawing a large circle on each sheet and colouring it red, amber and green.

Gather the young women together around the traffic light and hand each one a 'big night out' card. Each card should be read and then placed according to whether the reader thinks:

- Stop! That's dangerous! – RED
- That is a bit risky – AMBER
- That's fine! Go ahead! – GREEN

When all the cards have been placed, stopping to discuss the most dangerous ones first, consider those on amber. What could be done to make these situations less risky? Consider things that young women could do to make themselves as safe as possible to enjoy a night out. Agree, record and display these for future reference.

BIG NIGHT OUT CARDS

Make sure your mobile has credit and is fully charged before you go out	Accept a lift home with a friend of a friend	Set your mobile to vibrate when you walk home
Cut across the park alone after dark	Book a taxi home with friends before you go out	Sit in a train carriage with lots of other people in
Lie to parents / carers about where you are going	Make sure you save enough money for your bus fare home	Turn round and confront someone if you think they are following you
Keep your keys in your hand as you walk home	Keep your mobile in a separate pocket to your purse/wallet	Carry a knife for personal protection
Take Karate lessons so you can fight back	Chat to people you don't know on the way home	Drink so much you can't remember how you got home
Let a friend who is drunk walk home alone	Let someone pay for your drinks all night	Constantly check to see if you are being followed
Go back to someone's house the first night you meet them	Wear really uncomfortable shoes if you have to walk home	Carry a personal alarm
Walk with a group into town	Get into a car driven by someone who has been drinking	Call someone to come and get you if you feel frightened

4.6   Taking risks

This is a good introductory session to work around taking risks and risk-taking behaviour. It works best with groups of six to eight young women.

Aims

To promote discussion about risk-taking behaviour and how to reduce risks.

You will need

- a set of 'risk cards'
- two A4 sheets headed 'very risky' and 'not very risky'.

How to do it

Ask the young women to sit in a seated circle and hand each a risk card, asking them not to share what is on their card.

Place one of the A4 sheets on one side of the circle where everyone can see it and the other on the opposite side.

Explain that you want each young woman to read out what is on their card and then place the card where they think it should go between the two poles. So if they think what is on their card is 'very risky' then they should place their card nearest this end of the continuum or on the other side if they think it is 'not very risky'. They should then explain their decision. Stress that you are not asking if they have done it, just their opinion.

Set a rule that at this stage only the person who has the card can speak or make the decision, but there will be a chance later to challenge the choice.

Go around the circle until all the cards have been used and then invite the group to make any changes that they want. Once all the cards are in place discuss risk reduction. For example riding a motorbike may be more risky than driving a car, but one way to reduce risk would be to always wear a well-fitting crash helmet. Make sure that you explain that all risks are relative. Some effects of risky behaviour are immediate and could mean instant death, but some may not become obvious for years. For example being overweight as a young woman may not cause instant health problems, but could cause long-term problems later on in life.

RISK CARDS

Missing breakfast	Sleeping less than seven hours a night	Eating lots of red meat
Eating lots of fried food and chips	Not taking regular exercise	Smoking
Binge drinking alcohol at weekends	Misusing solvents	Not wearing a seat belt
Getting into a car when the driver has been drinking alcohol	Not using condoms	Being very overweight
Being very underweight	Vomiting after eating to diet	Not eating fruit or vegetables daily
Walking home alone at night	Not telling parents / carers where you are	Hanging around with young people who are in trouble with the police
Using Ecstasy at parties	Truanting from school / college	Smoking cannabis
Borrowing money when you can't pay it back	Playing hockey	Asking out someone you fancy

4.7   Sexually transmitted infections anagrams

This is a short activity to promote discussion and to assess the level of knowledge within a group.

Aim

To unscramble the anagrams and find the names of well-known sexually transmitted infections (STIs).

You will need

- copies of the 'anagram sheet' and pens
- STI leaflets and details of the local genito-urinary medicine (GUM) clinic.

How to do it

Divide the group into pairs and hand each couple an anagram sheet and a pen.

Tell the group they have ten minutes to work out the names of the sexually transmitted infections from the anagrams on their sheets.

Call time and then go through the answers checking out the young women's knowledge around each STI.

Reinforce how they can protect themselves to prevent contracting the infections and the names and numbers of local clinics that they should go to if they have concerns.

Distribute leaflets and identify areas for further work.

ANAGRAM SHEET – ANSWERS

1. Chlamydia
2. Genital warts
3. Herpes
4. Human immunodeficiency virus (HIV)
5. Gonorrhoea
6. Hepatitis B
7. Syphilis

ANAGRAM SHEET

1.   ADYIHCMAL

2.   RWSTA TIALENG

3.   PSREEH

4.   UMHAN MMIIEEIUNNODFCCY RUSIV

5.   EARROHOONG

6.   B EHPTTIISA

7.   IISLSYPH

4.8   Handshake

This is a quick, effective warm-up to use at the start of a session looking at STIs.

Aim

To illustrate to the group how easily STIs can be passed on.

You will need

- leaflets about different STIs
- details of your local GUM clinic.

How to do it

Invite two young women to step forward from the main group and shake hands and then rejoin the group.

Now ask all the young women, including the initial two, to stand up and shake the hand of the person standing next to them. Now ask them to shake the hand of the person on the other side of them, using the same hand.

Keep directing the group to repeat this until everyone has shaken hands with everyone else.

Finally announce that one of the first people to shake hands has got a sexually transmitted infection and that she has now been in contact with every member of the group. This should demonstrate how quickly an infection can be passed on and make the point that you can't always tell if someone is infected, as it is not something that can necessarily be seen.

Move on to discuss how STIs can be prevented and what a young woman should do if she thinks she is at risk of infection. Hand out information about local GUM clinics and make the point that these are confidential.

Answer any questions and assess the knowledge of the group for further sessions on sexual health.

4.9   STIs – the facts

This quiz is shown as an individual activity but if you know that you have members of your group who have low literacy skills you could adapt it to become a group activity.

Aim

To assess the young women's knowledge of STIs and to reinforce the need to use condoms.

You will need

- a copy of the quiz and a pen for each young woman
- leaflets about local GUM and family planning clinics or other places that distribute free condoms.

How to do it

Introduce the quiz, but make sure that you stress that you are not asking the young women if they are sexually active and that you do not expect them to know all the answers. Hand out the quiz sheet and pens and allow ten minutes (more if you have a larger group) for the young women to complete it. Ask that at this stage they do not talk to each other.

Go through the answers, answering questions and offering further information as requested. Encourage discussion and give out leaflets about local agencies and places where the young women can get free condoms if they require them. Reinforce any assertiveness work you have done and remind the young women that any sexual relationship should be consensual and remind them of the law.

This session can then lead on to further work around safe sex and positive relationships.

STIs – THE FACTS – ANSWERS

1. True.
2. True.
3. False – it stands for human immunodeficiency virus.
4. False – HIV is the virus that leads to AIDS.
5. True – around one third of these are undiagnosed.

6.   True – for the first time.

7.   True.

8.   False – many STIs (including chlamydia) don't have visible symptoms.

9.   False – new cases are common amongst the over 20s.

10. True.

11. False – some non-STIs have the same symptoms, for example cystitis can cause a burning sensation when passing urine but it is not sexually transmitted.

12. True.

13. True – it does help, but doesn't protect against things such as genital warts which are not covered by the condom.

STIs – THE FACTS – QUIZ[1]

		TRUE	FALSE	?
1.	Women aged 16–24 are at greatest risk of gonorrhoea infection.			
2.	Genital warts is the most common STI seen in GUM clinics.			
3.	HIV stands for human immune virus.			
4.	If you are HIV positive it means you have AIDS.			
5.	There are an estimated 49,500 people living with HIV/AIDS in the UK.			
6.	In 1999 the rate of heterosexually acquired HIV overtook the rate of HIV infections in men who have sex with men diagnosed in the UK.			
7.	Up to one in ten young woman have chlamydia.			
8.	You can tell if someone has an STI by looking at them.			
9.	New cases of herpes simplex are most common in people over 30.			
10.	Some symptoms are common to more than one STI.			
11.	There is no mistaking the symptoms of an STI.			
12.	The term STD is used less these days as 'infection' is a more accurate description than 'disease'.			
13.	Using condoms helps to prevent catching an STI.			

---

1 Information is taken from Brook, a national voluntary sector provider of free and confidential sexual health advice and services for young people under 25 (www.brook.org.uk).

4.10   How safe is safe?

This activity can be done with up to six young women. You will need to have built a good relationship for them to feel comfortable in participating. You will also need to be sensitive to the group's age and cultural background.

Aim

To look at what is meant by 'safe sex' in a confidential and supportive group. Leaflets and information about STIs and contraceptives can support this.

You will need

- small post-it notes
- pens
- two sheets of brightly coloured paper
- sexual health leaflets.

How to do it

On the two coloured sheets of paper write the words 'safe' and 'less safe' and place them about two metres apart on the floor.

Give each young woman a pen and three post-it notes. If you have a small group hand out more post-it pads. Ask the young woman to write on each paper a sexual act. Explain that they should do this individually and not show each other yet. Stress that you are not asking if they have done what they write down and that nobody will be questioned about their experiences.

When each young woman has completed the task take turns to place a paper between the 'safe' and 'less safe' poles. Once this has been done ask the group to consider if they feel all the papers are in the right place. They can then discuss with each other and agree a final sequence. For example 'kissing' should appear very close to 'safe' whereas 'unprotected sex' should be closest to the 'less safe' area.

4.11   STIs – a girl's guide

Aim

To offer young women information about the six most common sexually transmitted infections.[2]

You will need

- copies of the 'STIs information sheet' cut up

- envelopes

- leaflets about STIs and local GUM clinics

- additional cards or pieces of paper the same size as the boxes on the sheet.

How to do it

PREPARATION

Before the session enlarge the STIs information sheet and make photocopies. Then cut up and place each set into an envelope after shuffling the name, symptom and treatment cards. If you want to use the game again stick the cards onto A6 coloured card (approx 4 x 6") and laminate. Then cut up plain card (or paper) and place six blank cards into each envelope.

AT THE SESSION

Divide the main group into threes or fours. Explain that the activity is basically a sorting game. You are going to hand each group an envelope that has within it cards with the name, symptoms and treatment for six different STIs. Their task is to 'sort' the cards so that they match the right name with the correct symptoms and treatment. Stress that it doesn't matter if they are unsure or get it wrong.

Allow about 15 minutes and then ask the groups to stop. Go through and tell the young women the correct card order and discuss as you go along. Next hand out the leaflets and ask the young women to go through and find out one more thing about each of the STIs. They should then write their fact on one of the six blank cards in their pack.

Once everyone has completed the second part of the task, bring the whole group back together and invite them to share the additional facts that they have learnt.

Reinforce that using condoms greatly reduces the risk of transmitting STIs and make sure that the young women know where they can go locally to get them free.

---

2   Information is taken from Brook (www.brook.org.uk).

STIs INFORMATION SHEET

Name	Symptoms	Treatment
CHLAMYDIA	You can be unaware you are infected as there can be no symptoms. If there are these may include: unusual vaginal discharge, pain when passing urine, lower abdominal pain or abdominal pain during vaginal sex.	It is easily treated with antibiotics. Once the course of antibiotics is finished you should not have sex for another seven days to make sure the infection has cleared up and you don't pass it on.
Name	Symptoms	Treatment
HERPES SIMPLEX	Tingling or itching on or around the genital area followed by the appearance of small blisters, general flu-like symptoms and a burning sensation when passing urine.	There is no cure available but an anti-viral drug can reduce the severity of an episode and how long each episode lasts.
Name	Symptoms	Treatment
GONORRHOEA	Most women don't have any symptoms but you could notice unusual vaginal discharge, a burning feeling when passing urine, pain in your lower abdomen or heavy periods.	Antibiotics can cure gonorrhoea completely.
Name	Symptoms	Treatment
GENITAL WARTS	These are growths in the genital area that can appear up to a year after infection, but you may not see them if they are inside your vagina or anus.	Special ointment or paint is used to freeze the warts or they are removed surgically under local anaesthetic.

Name	Symptoms	Treatment
HIV	It may take ten or more years for you to develop symptoms, but the majority of people will eventually develop AIDS (acquired immune deficiency syndrome).	There is no cure for HIV or AIDS. Current treatment is a combination of three or more anti-viral drugs to try to maintain good health. However, the long-term outcome is still unclear.

Name	Symptoms	Treatment
HEPATITIS B	There may be no symptoms, but if there are they come in two stages between one and six months after infection. Stage 1: you feel flu-like with no appetite and painful joints. Stage 2: symptoms include jaundice, weight loss, and a sore abdomen.	There is no treatment apart from plenty of rest and a healthy diet. It usually takes several months to recover. There is a vaccine for people who know they are most at risk of catching hepatitis B.

4.12   Pass the parcel

This uses a familiar party game as a non-threatening method for introducing contraception and sexual health to a group.

Aim

The aim of the session is to gain a clearer understanding of the level of knowledge around contraception and sexual health within a group.

You will need

- a good selection of various methods of contraception
- appropriate leaflets and contact numbers
- newspaper or wrapping paper
- sticky tape
- music
- consent forms from parents to take part.

How to do it

PREPARATION

Before the young women arrive make a 'parcel' by wrapping layers of paper interspersed with the contraceptives you have collected. Make sure you and your colleagues are comfortable that you have enough information and knowledge of the contraceptives, how they work and their success rate to feel confident discussing any issues raised.

AT THE SESSION

Begin the activity by gathering the young woman together and asking them to sit down in a circle.

Bring out the parcel. Most of the group will have played 'pass the parcel' before, but for those who have not explain the rules.

As the music starts pass the parcel to the young woman on the left of you. The group should continue passing the parcel until the music stops.

The young woman holding the parcel when the music stops should then take off the first layer of paper and name the contraceptive and explain, if she can, how it works. At this point you may want to refer back to ground rules, such as confidentiality. It is a good idea to stress that you are not asking who has done or used what, nor do you expect the group to know all the answers. As each contraceptive is identified add additional information, for example the reliability of the method and whether it protects against STIs.

Repeat the process until all the layers are gone. Close the session by identifying areas that the group would like to look at further.

4.13   Pass it on!

This is an activity to use with six or more young women – the larger the group the more spectacular the results!

Aim

To raise awareness of the risks of unsafe sex and encourage young women to start to consider the consequences of choices and actions.

You will need

- a clear plastic cup for each young woman
- a dice (preferably a large one)
- water
- skimmed milk
- cornflour
- tincture of iodine (with a dropper in it).

How to do it

PREPARATION

Before the session you will need to make up a quantity of starch solution by mixing one level teaspoonful of cornflour thoroughly with a little cold water and then adding boiling water to make up a litre. Stir really well and then allow the mixture to cool. It should have a slightly milky cloudy appearance. Check a small amount by adding a few drops of iodine to it – it should turn dark blue or black!

Now prepare a clear plastic cup of water for each young woman in the group, all except one, with a small amount of skimmed milk in it to give the same appearance as the starch mix you already have. Make sure that each cup is the same colour and has the same amount in it.

Take the final empty cup and fill this to the same level as the others, but with the starch solution. Place all the cups onto a tray, checking again that all of them look the same.

THE ACTIVITY

As the young women come in invite each to take a plastic cup filled with liquid from the tray – make sure to tell them it isn't drinkable! Once everyone has one ask them to sit in a seated circle with their cup.

Place the dice in the middle and set these rules:

1. If a six is thrown the player chooses another member of the group to swap seats with.

2. If a four is thrown the person to the right of the player can choose to either tip a bit of the contents of their own cup into the dice thrower's cup, or to simply 'bump' cups and say 'Cheers!'

3. If a three is thrown the player should tip some out of their cup into another person's.

4. If a one is thrown the player chooses another member of the group to 'bump' cups with, saying 'Cheers!'

Ask for a volunteer to throw the dice first and keep going until the group have all had the opportunity to move around and interact with each other!

Now explain that actually the solutions in the beakers represented body fluids such as blood, semen or vaginal fluid.

- The six on the dice represents no sex – meeting someone new and talking to them.

- The four is the choice of whether to have penetrative sex or not. Adding to their neighbour's cup means they did. A 'Cheers!' means that they had safer sex.

- A three represents having penetrative unprotected sex.

- A one represents safer sex.

Explain that one of the cups had a marker in the 'body fluid' and was therefore able to cause an unplanned pregnancy or transmit an STI. Make the point that all the cups look the same – and still do.

Explain that you can now find out who has an unplanned pregnancy or STI by adding a few drops of the iodine solution to each cup. Add the iodine to each cup in turn and watch as the solutions change colour! This can be very dramatic.

Finally, once everyone can see the changes (if any) to their cup facilitate a discussion around the process. Can they guess yet who the 'infected' person is? If this were a real situation would it be easy to tell someone about an STI or unplanned pregnancy? Reinforce the need for safer sex and discuss options for young women concerned about STIs or pregnancies and where to go for help and support.

4.14   Healthy eating collage

This can be used with small groups of young women as an introductory session to look at healthy food. It can be supported with health authority leaflets on diet and fitness as appropriate. Any topics or concerns raised during the session can be identified for further work.

Aim

To raise the issue of healthy eating in a non-confrontational way and open up discussions around food.

You will need

- magazines
- scissors
- marker pens
- glue sticks
- flipchart paper.

How to do it

Split the group into two; set one group the task of looking through the magazines to find examples of healthy images of food and drink, the other the task of finding unhealthy images.

Then ask each group to take their images and make them into a collage on the flipchart paper. Agree that they can supplement the cuttings with words, slogans or feelings written with the marker pens. Bring the two groups back together to share their collages.

Ask questions to prompt discussion:

- How easy was it to find unhealthy/healthy options?
- Which looked more appealing?
- Were there lifestyles attached to images?
- What is the major difference between the people shown in each collage?

Then ask the group to look at their own eating habits. Ask each young woman to think of one healthy option they could choose to introduce to their lifestyle for the next week. This could be giving up smoking, cutting out sugar, limiting chocolate or walking to school. The youth workers will need to make a pledge too! Do try and encourage the young women to set realistic goals so that they can feel good about achieving it if they succeed, but not too embarrassed to come back if they don't!

Record the pledges on a sheet and keep for reviewing next week.

4.15   Food quiz

This quiz builds on the work started in the collage and encourages young women to think about what they eat and open discussions on dieting and eating healthily.

Aim

To give basic, correct information for young women to begin to make informed choices about the food they eat.

You will need

- copies of the quiz
- pens
- support leaflets and information (in case the session raises questions you can't answer).

How to do it

Hand out a copy of the quiz to each group member. If you know that some of the young women have difficulties with written exercises encourage them to work in pairs.

Allow about 15 minutes for them to look at the questions and consider their answers. Each question consists of a statement to consider, and they should choose which of the three options (a), (b) or (c) fits this statement best. Ask them to work individually or in their pairs without reference to other members at this stage.

FOOD QUIZ – ANSWERS

1c, 2a, 3c, 4b, 5b, 6a, 7c, 8b, 9c, 10b (source: www.need2know.co.uk/health)

Go through the questions and answers with the group discussing responses. Reinforce healthy eating options and the need for a balanced diet and regular exercise, handing out leaflets where appropriate.

FOOD QUIZ

1. There are two main types of food: 'good' and 'bad'.

   (a) Vegetarian food is 'good' food and by far the healthiest option. It would be best to give up eating meat, which is bad for you.

   (b) To be healthy you should give up eating 'bad' food like chips and bread and eat 'good' food like lentils and beans.

   (c) No food is 'good' or 'bad'. The important bit is to balance food from the five food groups – including five portions of fruit and vegetables a day.

2. Eating carbohydrates like bread, potatoes and pasta will make you put on weight so you should avoid them.

   (a) No – these foods fill you up and give you energy; just avoid frying or adding butter.

   (b) Yes – these foods should be avoided as they are high in calories and low in nutritional value.

   (c) Yes – these foods are high in fat so should be limited to once a week.

3. 100g of French fries contain more fat than a jacket potato.

   (a) True – 100g French fries contains 20g of fat compared to a 100g baked potato that contains less than 1g.

   (b) True – but only just! 100g of French fries contains 3g of fat compared to a 100g baked potato that contains 2g.

   (c) True – 100g of French fries contains 15g fat compared to a 100g jacket potato that contains less than 1g.

4. There is no point in drinking skimmed milk – all the goodness has gone!

   (a) Skimmed milk has less calcium and protein than whole milk as it is lost in the skimming process.

   (b) All milk is a good source of calcium and protein. When milk is skimmed it is only fat that is removed.

(c) During the skimming process the milk is heated to boiling point before being cooled in huge coolers. It is during this process that protein is destroyed although there is still calcium left in the milk.

5. Frozen vegetables don't count towards your five a day.

   (a) True – most of the vitamins are destroyed in the freezing process.

   (b) False – frozen vegetables all retain their vitamins and minerals when they are frozen.

   (c) Depends – on which vegetables and fruit it is. Freezing destroys the vitamins in some delicate vegetables, such as peas. This means you would have to eat four times the amount of frozen peas to get the same amount of vitamins and minerals you get in a portion of fresh peas.

6. Which of these is an oily fish that is a good source of unsaturated (Omega 3) fat?

   (a) Salmon.

   (b) Cod.

   (c) Eel.

7. It is best to be on the safe side and take vitamin supplements to make sure you get enough vitamins daily.

   (a) Yes – no matter how well you eat you can never have too many vitamins.

   (b) It is a good way to avoid being ill by boosting the number of vitamins you take daily.

   (c) If you eat a balanced, varied diet you shouldn't need to take anything extra to keep you healthy.

8. Very low calorie ready meals are an excellent way to lose weight fast.

   (a) True – eat three low calorie ready meals a day and you will be thinner and healthier.

   (b) False – very low calorie diets don't provide enough energy for healthy growth and ready meals can contain way too much salt.

(c)   True – and eating only meal replacement shakes works even better.

9. If it is hot you should add more salt to your food to make up for salt lost through sweating.

(a)   Only if you like salt.

(b)   Only rock sea salt as this is purer.

(c)   Most UK diets include more salt than the body needs so even in hot weather you don't need extra.

10. Adding bran to food is a good way to get enough fibre.

(a)   True – it is really good for your digestion.

(b)   Not a good idea as it may upset your stomach. It is better to choose wholemeal pasta, bread and eat plenty of fruit, vegetables and pulses such as beans and lentils.

(c)   True – you can't really have too much fibre in your diet.

4.16   Health services treasure hunt

This is a great way to encourage young women to find information and introduce agencies to them. You will need to do a risk assessment and obtain parental consent so allow time for this in advance.

Aim

The aim of the activity is to collect information about a wide range of health support agencies.

You will need

- 'health services treasure hunt' sheets
- pens
- travel passes
- travel maps
- phone cards/emergency phone money
- packed lunches and drinks (the young women should bring these)
- a prize!

How to do it

BEFORE THE DAY

In advance of the health services treasure hunt you will need to make contact with the agencies that you are planning to use and agree with them to take part. Explain that you need a nominated person to meet the young women as they arrive to tell them about the agency and then hand them a signed leaflet or card to prove that they have visited. Alternatively, you may choose to do this as a 'mystery shopping' exercise to find out what local health services for young people offer and the service they get.

This is a whole day event, so you will need to identify several agencies. These could include:

- GUM clinic
- local pharmacy
- Youth Enquiry and Information Shop or Connexions One-Stop-Shop
- family planning clinic
- mobile health project.

You will also need to prepare a 'health services treasure hunt sheet' that has all the names, addresses and contact numbers of the agencies, a space for notes and tick boxes for the young women to complete as they go along.

Once this is done you will need to send out parental consent forms (for under 18s) and complete a risk assessment. On the information you send out stress that the young women will either need a packed lunch and drinks or money for snacks on the day. You will also need an emergency contact for the day agreed in case parents need to get hold of the young women. This could be yourself, but it may be a good idea to find someone at the youth office to do this for you.

Decide on a prize to give the young women who return to the agreed end point first – preferably something healthy!

Finally, once you know how many young women are going to take part in the day buy travel passes for local buses or trains (if necessary) and obtain a map of the area.

ON THE DAY

Meet the young women and divide them into pairs. Explain that their challenge is to find and visit as many of the agencies as possible on the health services treasure hunt sheet and return to the designated end point. During the visit they should find out about the agency and collect at least three leaflets, one of which will need to be signed as 'proof' of the visit. The winners of the challenge are the first pair to return with the most information and signed sheets.

Hand out maps, lists, pens and an emergency phone card/money and a contact number that the young women can call if there is a problem. Make sure you keep a copy of all their emergency contact details and parental consent forms. Check also that you have correct mobile numbers and that everyone has food, drink or money on them before they set off.

Award the prize to the winning pair! Then once everyone is back ask each pair to give feedback on one agency thinking about the following:

- How easy was it to find?
- How young people 'friendly' is the agency?
- What services do they offer?
- Are the leaflets/information sheets clear and easily understood?
- Would they recommend the service to other young women?

Finally ask each person to make a positive comment about the presentations made and close the day. Make a display of agency leaflets as a reminder and to refer to in other sessions.

4.17 Drugs Jenga

This activity uses a well-known game and adapts it to look at drugs issues. As the questions are random it is possible to discuss attitudes and knowledge and assess skills in a non-personal way.

Aim

To remove wooden bricks from the Jenga tower and answer questions.

You will need

- one wooden Jenga game (a Milton Bradley game) on which you have written the drugs questions
- black permanent marker pen
- a flat, level surface.

How to do it

TO CREATE THE GAME

Write with a black permanent marker on random Jenga blocks the name of a drug or a question from the list given on the next page. You can add your own to meet the needs of the young women playing. The questions will help open up discussions around attitudes to drug taking in the group and check out skills.

TO PLAY THE GAME

Build the Jenga blocks into a high tower. Each player in turn, including the youth workers, removes one block from the stack of Jenga blocks without knocking the whole thing over. If it has a question on then she should read it out loud and answer and then replace the block at the top of the tower. If she pulls out the name of a drug she should tell the group three things she knows about that drug and then put the block back on top. If a blank block is pulled out then she should just place the block back into the top of the tower.

If a player is uncomfortable about answering any question, she can put the block on top without answering, but must then take another block.

If a player pulls a block she has already answered, she must also pull another one.

If a player knocks the whole thing over, the game is finished and all the other players get to choose any of the questions to ask her before rebuilding the tower and starting again.

DRUGS JENGA – QUESTIONS AND NAMES

COCAINE	CANNABIS	ECSTASY
SKUNK	MAGIC MUSHROOMS	CRACK
HEROIN	SOLVENTS	LSD
AMPHETAMINE	CAFFEINE	TRANQUILLISERS
What are some of the health risks for injecting drugs?	If a friend collapses after using drugs what should you do?	Why do you think it can be dangerous to mix drugs?
What can you do to prevent your drink being 'spiked'?	What class drug is cannabis?	Which common drinks contain the stimulant caffeine?
Name some of the solvents that can be found in most homes.	Why is dehydration a problem for ecstasy users?	What are the dangers of using solvents alone?

Do you think there is a link between drug use and unsafe sex? Why?	Who could you tell if you were worried about a friend's drug use?	What should you do if you find used needles and syringes?
What are the dangers of exceeding the dosage of paracetamol?	Name three illegal substances.	Someone offers you a lift home, but you know they have been smoking cannabis – what do you do?
What is the difference between cocaine and crack?	What would you tell a friend who wants to try Ecstasy for the first time?	What is the difference between cannabis and skunk?
What are the names of some commonly prescribed tranquillisers?	What does LSD usually look like?	Do you think most young people try illegal drugs at some point?
Tell us some of the street names used for cannabis.	What is cocaine often called?	What could you do if someone offered you a drug and you didn't want to try it?

Chapter 5

Positive Relationships

5.1   Friendship lines

This is a good way to look at friendships past and present and the importance of them to our personal 'history'.

Aim

To encourage each young woman to create a friendship line showing their important female friendships and the role they play in their lives.

You will need

- sheets of flipchart paper
- marker pens
- glitter/sequins/material and any other decorations you have.

How to do it

Hand each young woman a sheet of flipchart paper and place a good selection of markers close by.

Explain to the group that they are each going to make a 'friendship line' to depict female friends who are, or who have been, important to them from their earliest memories to the present. They can use words or pictures and if they want to bring in photos to add to it this can be done too.

Whilst explaining the task, stress that it is up to individuals to choose how much they wish to put onto paper and share. Also point out that it does not matter how many or few people are recorded on the line – this is an exercise to look at friendships and what they mean, not a competition to see who knows the most people.

Once everyone has finished ask the young women to come together and share highlights of their friendship line. Are there similarities? Has everyone kept in touch with early friends? Are some friendships associated with different activities or clubs? Do friends have different roles in their lives? For example is there someone who always makes them laugh or always listens? Go on to discuss what it is that makes a friend special.

5.2   My awards

Aim

To consider important relationships, what makes them so special, and how they contribute to our personal world view.

You will need

- paper and pens
- an ornament or statue to use as an award
- film extracts of an award ceremony.

How to do it

Show the clip or clips of an award ceremony that you have chosen. If you can find one that shows an emotional acceptance even better!

Once everyone has watched the film, suggest that at award ceremonies people want to thank everybody who has contributed to their success, from business associates to relatives.

Now, ask the young women to imagine that they have just won an award and will be attending a glittering award ceremony. Who would they want to thank for making a positive contribution to their lives and why? This should be someone that they feel has influenced their beliefs and values as they have grown up and needs to be something that they are happy to share with the group.

Hand out the paper and pens and invite them to write their acceptance speech. This should be short, but include their thanks.

Whilst the young women do this, arrange the chairs around a clear space, which will become the stage area. If you have lights or a microphone available you could set this up to make the set even more authentic.

Once everyone has finished, invite the young women into the theatre area you have prepared. Explain that only those on 'stage' will be talking, the rest will form the audience. Encourage someone to go first to read their speech and accept their award from you. Make sure you introduce everyone and lead a round of applause as they go onto and leave the stage.

When the last girl has spoken, thank everyone for coming and close the award ceremony in true TV presenter style!

Bring the group into a circle and review how it felt to publicly thank people. Facilitate a discussion that explores further the impact family members, both living and historical, have on personal beliefs and values.

5.3   Gender game

This is an opportunity to explore the concept that boys want sex and girls want love, by encouraging empathy and understanding.

Aim

To discuss feelings across the gender divide in a non-threatening way.

You will need

- copies of the 'gender game cards'
- a sheet of flipchart paper for each group
- markers.

How to do it

Demonstrate drawing a Venn diagram (two overlapping circles), and label one circle 'Male', one circle 'Female' and the bit where they cross in the middle 'Both'.

Divide the main group into fives or sixes and hand each group a pack of gender game cards and a flipchart sheet and marker. Ask each group to copy your diagram onto their sheet. Now, explain that the group task is to discuss each card in turn and then place it in the area that they think is true. So, for example if they think that it is mainly women who worry about pregnancy they should place the card in the 'Female' zone, if they think it is mainly men, then it goes in the 'Male' zone. If they think it is of equal concern to both genders then it goes in the 'Both' section. Point out that there are no right or wrong answers.

Allow about 20 minutes for discussion and then rotate around the groups asking each for one their decisions and reasons. Spend time discussing cards that have been placed in different areas, asking the young women to consider if it really is 'different for girls', and if so why. Reinforce the point that young men have feelings too and that some of the pressures that girls feel are reflected in male concerns. Suggest that in positive relationships, where both partners can talk and discuss feelings, misconceptions and misunderstandings are less likely.

GENDER GAME CARDS

Worry about pregnancy	Spend a lot of time worrying about relationships
Want to remain a virgin until they are married	Want to use condoms
Think that having lots of money makes you more sexually attractive	Think it is OK to have lots of one night stands
Want to feel loved before they have sex	Want to have a family
Feel pressured into having sex	Want to have more than one sexual partner at a time
Worry what their partners think	Get hurt feelings
Shout at their partners	Hit their partners
Learn about sex from magazines	Have to be drunk to want sex
Worry about what their friends think	Worry that they may not be good in bed
Worry about the size/ shape of their bodies	Worry about oral sex

5.4   Sex and the media

Aim

To reflect on the power of the media and the messages given about sex and relationships.

You will need

- marker pens
- four sheets of flipchart paper
- a good selection of magazines.

How to do it

To prepare for the exercise look through a wide selection of magazines and find adverts that feature attractive men and women selling products. This can be anything from cars to food. Cut them out and if you have access to a laminator, laminate them.

Divide the young women into four groups and give each group a selection of the adverts, some pens and a sheet of flipchart paper to work with. Using a marker, the paper should be divided in to four sections and headed:

1. What product or service is advertised?
2. Who is the advert aimed at?
3. How do the models look?
4. Are there any hidden messages?

Allow time for discussion and then invite feedback, particularly focusing on the 'hidden messages'. For example: this product is for couples; all young people are having sex; men have to be strong and tough; only thin women are sexually attractive. Discuss how true these messages are and how representative they are of 'real life' relationships.

5.5　Healthy relationships

Aim

This activity helps young women to consider what a healthy relationship is and also to reflect on some of the indicators of a less healthy one.

You will need

- sets of the 'relationship cards' (enough for the young women to work in threes or fours)

- envelopes to put the cards in

- two extra cards for each pack – one marked 'being in a healthy relationship' and one marked 'being in an unhealthy relationship'.

How to do it

Divide the young women up into smaller groups of three or four, and explain that they will be working together for the next session looking at healthy relationships. Explain that as this is a subject that may bring up personal feelings and emotions it is a good idea to discuss the main group contract already in place and add any extra 'rules' that will enable their smaller group to feel comfortable sharing and discussing.

Allow about five minutes for this to happen and then hand out the packs of relationship cards, one pack per group. Explain that inside their packs the young women will find cards with different statements on them. They will also see two cards, 'being in a healthy relationship' and 'being in an unhealthy relationship'. The task is to discuss each of the statements and then as a group decide if each card should go onto the 'healthy' or 'unhealthy' relationship pile. If there are cards that they cannot agree on then ask that the young women put these to one side for further discussion later.

After about 20 minutes check to see how the groups are getting on, allowing more time if needed. Invite each group to offer a point from their 'healthy' pile, encouraging discussion as you go round. Then ask the young women to share a card from their 'unhealthy' pile asking them to clarify why they feel it is negative and inviting additional comments from the rest of the groups.

Finally, ask the groups to share any that they were uncertain where to place. Discuss these in more detail, especially if other groups have placed these already on a pile. Ask the young women to reach a group consensus before moving on to look at strategies the young women can use to promote healthy relationships for themselves.

RELATIONSHIP CARDS

Respecting each other and allowing each person to be themselves	Spending time doing things with friends and family away from each other
One person taking charge and making all the decisions	Telling lies about where you have been or who you have been with
Thinking your partner has 'gone off' you if they want to spend time alone	Feeling jealous if your partner talks to someone else
Telling your friends details of your sexual relationship with your partner	Apologising for your partner all the time in front of friends
Listening to each other's feelings, hopes and dreams	Being honest about your sexual history and sexual health status with each other
Feeling scared to ask your partner to use a condom	Feeling not as 'good' as your partner
Texting all the time as you can't bear to be apart	Pretending to be on the pill when you are not

RELATIONSHIP CARDS

Needing to know where your partner is all the time	Feeling you have to justify yourself all the time
Resolving arguments by talking even when you feel really angry	Feeling 'trapped' but unable to end the relationship
Having sex even when you don't want to	Not seeing your best mate as much because your partner doesn't like them
Respecting and caring for yourself before and during a relationship	Respecting sexual boundaries and the right to say 'no'
Constantly needing your partner to tell you they love you	Shouting, shoving or hitting when you argue
Seeing someone else at the same time as your partner	Agreeing to non-penetrative sex until you both feel ready

5.6 'No means no' quiz

This quiz can be used with both individual young women and in small groups. Make sure that you know if any members of the group have been the victim of rape or sexual assault before you decide if it is appropriate to use.

Aim

Use this quiz to assess attitudes towards sexual violence and rape and to open up discussions around staying safe.

You will need

- a copy of the quiz and a pen for each young woman
- leaflets about local GUM clinics and rape crisis centres
- information about local police.

How to do it

Ask the young women to tell you what they think is meant by the term 'rape'; point out that not all rape is committed by men on women – men can be the victims of rape too.

Hand out the quiz and ask the young women to read the statements and put a tick if they agree with the statement in the end box, a cross if they don't agree or a question mark if they are unsure.

Once everyone has completed the sheet discuss the answers. Facilitate a discussion as points are raised and make sure you stress the following:

- If a woman is forced to have intercourse against her will it is always rape.
- Everyone has the right to say 'no' regardless of the circumstances.
- 'Date rape' is rape by someone that the victim knows or has met and may even have a romantic relationship with.
- Even if you have enjoyed the start of the sexual encounter but refuse to go further it is still rape if you are forced.

Now move on to look at ways that young women can protect themselves against sexual assault or reduce risk. This should include things such as not walking home alone, telling people where they are, not getting into situations where they are alone and vulnerable with young men they have just met, being clear about their sexual boundaries and feeling assertive enough to say 'no'.

Conclude the session by explaining where the young women can go for help if they are the victims of sexual assault or rape and give out details of local support agencies. Plan any additional work that needs to be done with the group for future sessions.

✔

'NO MEANS NO' QUIZ

		TRUE	FALSE	?
1.	If a young man is drunk it isn't rape if he forces you to have sex because he is out of control and not responsible for his actions.			
2.	The way some girls dress makes boys think they want sex.			
3.	Having sex with a woman if she is too drunk or drugged to say yes or no is not considered rape.			
4.	Keeping your drink with you at all times in pubs or clubs will stop someone putting something in your drink.			
5.	If you say you will have sex with someone you should go through with it even if you change your mind.			
6.	When rape happens on a date it is usually because the girl wants to have sex but is scared that people will call her a slag.			
7.	If you have already had sex with someone before it is not really rape if you refuse.			
8.	You can tell if someone is a rapist by the way they look and behave.			
9.	If you are raped and call the police they won't believe you if it is someone you know.			
10.	Unwanted pregnancy is the main thing to worry about if you are raped.			
11.	Every woman has a responsibility to herself to keep out of sexually risky situations.			
12.	If you get into bed with someone it is your own fault if they assume you want sex.			

5.7   I said 'NO!'

This activity follows on well from the previous one and is suitable for small groups of young women.

Aim

To provide an opportunity to experiment with different ways of saying 'no'.

You will need

- a copy of the 'I said "no!" sheet' for each young woman
- a copy of the 'scenarios' sheets cut up.

How to do it

Introduce the session and refer to your group contract before you start. Ask the young women to choose a partner to work with, or randomly divide them up if you want them to work with someone they may not usually choose.

Hand out a copy of the 'I said "no!" sheet' and a scenario to each young woman.

Now explain that in their pairs they are going to take turns in role-playing the scenario, using the sheet to try out different ways to say 'no' to what their partner is asking them to do.

Allow about 20 minutes for each pair to work through their role-play before bringing the whole group back together again.

Facilitate a discussion that looks at how easy it was to say 'no', what techniques were most effective and examples of this which could be reflected in their own experiences or potential situations.

I SAID 'NO!' SHEET

Verbal ways to say no:

- Say 'no' and leave it at that.

- Say 'no' and repeat it over and over.

- Say 'no' and give a reason.

- Say 'no' and give an excuse.

- Say 'no' and suggest an alternative.

- Say 'no' and laugh it off as a joke.

Non-verbal ways of saying no:

- Use your body to signal 'no' – stand back, hold up your hands, shake your head.

- Use your face to signal 'no' – make a face, frown, look disgusted.

I SAID 'NO!' – SCENARIOS

(1) Sarah has been waiting all week to go on her first date with Joe on Friday night. She is really nervous and decides to raid the fridge and steal some of her mum's vodka to give her courage before she goes. As she gets ready she thinks about how much she likes Joe and before she knows it she has drunk a quarter of the bottle with diet cola.

When Joe arrives she realises that she is drunk and a bit unsteady on her feet. On the way to the club Joe pulls out another bottle of vodka and offers her a drink. Sarah wants to refuse, she knows that she has drunk enough, but is scared that he will laugh at her, especially as she is three years younger than him.

(2) Tom and Lucy have been seeing each other a while and have kissed but not had sex yet. Tonight they are in his bedroom alone and things are moving on, but Lucy still doesn't feel ready to have full sex. Tom keeps trying to put his hand up Lucy's skirt but she keeps moving away. Finally he says, 'Come on Lucy, relax – you know I love you. Let's smoke this and see if it helps you chill out a bit.' He reaches into his pocket and brings out a joint, then lights it.

Lucy doesn't know what to do – she likes Tom a lot but she doesn't want to do this.

(3) Joel has taken Jenny out for dinner and is giving her a lift home. Suddenly he pulls over into the car park of the local park. It is dark and she can see that no one is around.

Joel turns to Jenny and suggests they climb into the back. She hesitates and he says, 'Come on – I want to show you how much I fancy you!' When she shakes her head and asks him to take her home he says, 'What? But I paid for your dinner! Aren't you going to thank me properly?' Jenny really doesn't want to but doesn't know what to say.

(4) Charlotte is babysitting and has called her boyfriend Eddie and asked him to join her. They have had a really nice evening together but the TV is now boring and they are wondering what to watch next. Charlotte suggests a DVD, but Eddie says he hasseen all the films on the shelf. Suddenly he starts sniggering and suggests they watch the Adult Channel. Charlotte is angry; isn't she enough for Eddie? Why does he want to watch porn? When she challenges him Eddie looks scornful. 'You are such a goody-goody!' he says. 'Everyone watches porn – it will get us in the mood for some fun of our own!'

Charlotte panics and wonders what she should do. She doesn't like the idea at all but doesn't want Eddie to think she is no fun and dump her.

(5) Kayleigh has been sleeping with Darren for months and she is happy to be in a long-term relationship. Her friends don't like him as he has a reputation for fighting but Kayleigh doesn't care because she knows that he would never hurt her.

Tonight they are at his house and his parents are out. 'Let's go to bed!' suggests Darren and takes Kayleigh's hand to lead her upstairs. Usually she does what he wants but tonight she replies, 'I can't, I've got my period at the moment, sorry.' Darren looks angry. 'I don't mind,' he says firmly pulling on her hand harder, 'I want to anyway.' Kayleigh feels worried; she has really bad stomach cramps and just wants to go home. She would be happy to cuddle him but when she starts to say this he cuts in and says, 'I'm warning you – don't make me angry!' She looks at him and starts to feel nervous. What can she do? She hates it when he is aggressive with her, even though he says he can't help it and is always sorry later.

(6) Jasmine met Ravi tonight and she is really happy! All her mates fancy him but he has made it clear that it is her he is interested in. As the lights go up he offers to walk her home and she excitedly waves her friends goodbye – this is even better than she expected, now she won't have to say good night for at least another half hour!

As they walk home hand in hand she feels really pleased – he has already said he wants to see her again. As they walk through the park he turns to kiss her and she closes her eyes in anticipation. A few minutes later he starts to unbutton her top. 'Wait a minute,' Jasmine says breathlessly, 'I am not sure about this.' Ravi stands back and frowns. 'What's up?' he asks. 'You've been coming onto me all night! Don't go shy on me now!' Jasmine starts to panic; she suddenly realises she is alone in a dark park with someone she doesn't know. Ravi starts to touch her again. Jasmine wonders what to do; she does like him and would like to see him again but she isn't ready to have sex now.

5.8   Relationship pyramid

Aim

The aim of this activity is to encourage discussion about the personal attributes and qualities that young women may value in the people that they choose to have relationships with. There are no right or wrong answers for this activity – it is all down to personal priorities!

You will need

- sets of the 'relationship pyramid cards'.

How to do it

The task for each group is to read the attributes on the cards included in the pack, discuss how important each is in a potential partner and then agree a 'pyramid' of importance for the cards included in the pack. Each group forms a pyramid, which they have to discuss and agree. It should end up with five cards along the bottom row, then four, three, two and finally one at the top. Remember the whole group has to agree their final pyramid!

Allow about 20 minutes for the pyramids to be agreed. When everyone is happy with their cards, place them on the floor in front of the group.

Now, look at the pyramids. Are they all the same? Where there are differences ask the group to share their thinking behind the decisions as far as they are comfortable. Facilitate any discussion and encourage the young women to challenge decisions, ensuring that this does not become an opportunity for personal attacks on individual values.

RELATIONSHIP PYRAMID CARDS

Has a good body	Is a good laugh	Has lots of mates
Listens to me	Has a brain	Is good looking
Does not talk behind my back	Someone who I am proud to be with	Is not afraid to show me how they feel
Chooses to spend time with me	Does not show off to friends	Cares what I think
Makes an effort with personal hygiene	Someone I can trust	Someone my friends like

5.9   Gender stereotypes and relationships

Aim

To examine how gender stereotypes can affect relationships.

You will need

- a copy of the 'scenarios' sheet.

How to do it

Explain to the young women that in this session you are going to explore situations where gender roles and stereotypes might affect relationships.

Divide the larger group into smaller ones of three or four and hand a scenario to each group. One young woman should read out the scenario and then facilitate a group discussion using the questions at the bottom. Explain that the task is to find an agreed way to resolve the issues.

Allow about ten minutes for the discussion and another five to reach agreement and then ask for a volunteer to speak from each group to the large group.

Invite the volunteers to take it in turns to outline their scenario and the issues they considered before reaching a decision on how to resolve the situation. Set a ground rule that no one from other groups can comment until after the group has finished speaking. After that allow two to three minutes for the other young women to comment or debate. When all the groups have taken their turn to present, facilitate a short discussion that considers the following:

1. Are there traditional gender roles within all relationships? If so what are they and how do they impact on how the relationships interact?

2. Do males or females have more 'power' in a relationship? How?

3. Are any stereotypes the same for older generations, for example parents?

4. How do cultural values or beliefs impact on these gender roles?

GENDER STEREOTYPES AND RELATIONSHIPS – SCENARIOS

(1) Craig is about to ask Michelle out for the first time when she walks over to him and says, 'Hi Craig! There's a new club open in town and I really want to go. Are you going on Saturday? We could go together.' Craig was planning to ask her to go with him but he wants to be the one to do the asking. He thinks that he will say he is going with his mates.

- Do you think it is OK for Michelle to ask Craig out?

- Why do you think he is going to tell her he is going with his friends?

- What would you do if you were Michelle?

(2) Emma has just been offered an apprenticeship with a local plumber and she is really pleased. She tells John, her boyfriend, 'I am so excited! This is just what I always wanted – to be taken seriously as a trainee plumber!' John doesn't look pleased and frowns when she asks him if there is something wrong. 'Look,' he says, 'I don't want to go out with a plumber! You are going to have to make a choice: me, or the apprenticeship!'

- What should Emma do?

- Why do you think John has a problem with Emma's career choice?

- What reactions do you think she will get from other friends and her family?

(3) Sam wants to buy a doll for her three-year-old nephew's birthday. She knows he will love it and thinks it is great that he is so caring. When she tells her boyfriend, Tia, her plans he looks disgusted. 'You can't do that!' Tia explodes. 'He is a boy! Boys don't play with dolls – get him a train or something!' Sam is confused. 'But my nephew asked for a doll, he doesn't like trains, what's the problem?'

- What do you think Tia is worried about if the little boy is given a doll for his birthday?

- What do you think – are some toys gender specific?

- What reactions do you think the present might arouse in other family members?

5.10   Family messages

This is the first of a two-part programme that explores values. It is best to use with an established group of young women who feel comfortable discussing thoughts and feelings.

Aim

To identify values learnt from families and to explore personal values.

You will need

- copies of the 'family messages sheet'
- pens.

How to do it

Begin the session by checking out the young women's understanding of the concept 'values', suggesting that values are our concepts of what is right, worthwhile or desirable. Stress that these qualities, principles and beliefs are important to us and go towards informing our 'world view' of how things are or should be.

Next, ask the young women to consider where their values come from. Are we born with them or do we learn them from the people around us? Suggest that family and close relationships inform our values and what we believe and ask the young women to think about values being passed down through generations.

Hand out the family messages sheets with pens and ask the young women to spend a few minutes looking through it and then filling it in. Ask that they do this individually at the moment, explaining that there will be an opportunity to share later.

Now, split the main group into smaller groups of threes or fours and invite the young women to share information on each topic. Do these reflect her personal beliefs? How easy is it to challenge values that she doesn't hold at home?

Ask the smaller groups to pick out a few main points from their conversations to share in the main group. As a whole group share issues raised and then conclude with a short discussion:

1. Are there family values that are not openly discussed, but everyone knows? How are these messages communicated?

2. Do the men in the family get a different message from the women?

3. Are there family messages that the young women want to pass on to any children they have/may have?

4. Are there any family values that they will not communicate to future generations?

FAMILY MESSAGES SHEET

Doing well at school/college

Messages:

Getting a good job and earning money

Messages:

Drugs and alcohol

Messages:

Sexual relationships

Messages:

Having children

Messages:

Breaking the law

Messages:

Having a car or driving

Messages:

Having expensive clothes

Messages:

Friendships

Messages:

Telling the truth

Messages:

5.11   Exploring personal values

This follows on from the previous activity and is suitable for small groups or individual work.

Aim

To produce a 'map' that explores personal values and beliefs.

You will need

- large sheets of paper
- coloured felt pens.

How to do it

Explain to the young women that the purpose of this session is to produce a 'map' that clearly shows the values and beliefs that are important to them. Stress that we all hold different values and that there are no right or wrong answers to this activity, as long as it doesn't put down another group member or make them feel uncomfortable.

Invite the young women to choose a coloured pen to represent themselves and then draw a 'dot' or person in the middle of the page. Explain that it doesn't matter if they are not the best artists in the world – as long as they are happy that it now shows where they sit in the middle of their world.

Now, using a different colour, ask the young women to write value statements around the central figure. If you know that they are not comfortable with writing tasks suggest that they draw pictures to show what they feel. Explain that values that they feel strongly about, for example 'being loyal to friends' or 'being honest', should be shown close to their symbol. Those values that they hold but that are not so important should be shown further away from themselves on the map. Allow about ten minutes, to think through the process and map everything.

Once all the young women have finished, use the map as a discussion point. Ask questions and explore values, but make sure that you refer to the group contract, reinforcing that you support the behaviour of standing up for personal values, without necessarily sharing them. This will be especially important if controversial issues are raised in the group or there are differing viewpoints. For example, contraception, abortion or politics might be controversial.

Encourage the young women to take ownership of what they are saying by using 'I' statements and ensure that everyone is given the space to talk. Highlight shared beliefs as well as those that the young women feel differently about.

Go on to discuss how people may stick up for their beliefs or protest if they feel these are being disrespected, challenged or ignored.

5.12   Anger and violence explored

This is a good opening session to look at anger and issues around violent behaviour with small groups of young women.

Aim

To identify links between anger and violent behaviour and consider ways to manage anger non-violently.

You will need

- flipchart paper and markers
- newspaper cuttings that report on violent incidents
- Blu-Tack.

How to do it

Start off by acknowledging that anger is a valid emotion or response to certain situations and that everyone feels angry sometimes. Emphasise that it is not the emotion that sometimes causes problems but how we react to it and behave.

Suggest that anger is a common cause of violence amongst young people and ask the young women to idea storm some of the factors that may cause this, for example:

- wanting to feel powerful
- losing control
- alcohol or drug misuse
- having a 'hard' reputation to maintain.

Record these on a sheet of flipchart paper and leave it up where the young women can see it during the session.

Now ask the young women to close their eyes and think back to the last time they felt really angry. This may have been an incident related to money, an argument with parents, a friend or someone else that made them feel disrespected or a situation at school. Encourage the young women to really concentrate on the memory, thinking about what led up to the incident and then remember the feelings that arose as they became angry.

After a couple of minutes invite the young women to open their eyes and take it in turns to describe how they felt when they became frustrated or angry during the situation they have been thinking about. Encourage them to describe the physical sensations, for example breathing hard, going red in the face, rapid heartbeat or becoming tearful. List these on a fresh sheet and then move on to psychological sensations, for example feeling out of control, feeling like hitting someone, feeling like you will explode.

Once you have a full list, write a title 'How I feel when I am angry' in a different coloured marker and stick that up.

Now ask the young women to think of things they actually do when they get angry. Stress this is different to 'feel like doing'. List these up under the heading 'What I do when I am angry', and stick the sheet up next to the feelings list.

In groups of three or four ask the young women to look at the list and consider the differences between the two lists. Ask them to pull out three main points from their conversations to share with everyone.

After 10 to 15 minutes bring the whole group back together and take the points from each group, encouraging discussion as you go. If no one makes the point add that 'feelings' don't hurt anyone else, but 'actions' do.

Conclude the discussion by considering ways to manage feelings so that they do not result in violent actions: for example, walking away from the situation. Put these ideas up on a sheet as well and place it next to the first two sheets to refer to in future sessions.

5.13   Passive, assertive, aggressive

Aim

To explore passive, aggressive and assertive behaviour and consider alternative ways of expressing feelings.

You will need

- a flipchart sheet with a drawing of a thermometer on it – this will be the 'anger thermometer'
- post-it notes and pens.

How to do it

Divide the young women into threes. Ask each small group to discuss soap operas that they watch and the way that the actors portray feeling angry. Encourage them to think in particular about behaviour and consequences. Then hand out post-it notes to each group and ask them to write the name of a soap character on each one.

Now, show the young women the 'anger thermometer' you have put onto the wall. Explain that the thermometer is a continuum, with 'passive' at one end of the scale, through 'assertive' to 'aggressive' at the far end. Offer these broad definitions to help:

- passive: not expressing your own feelings or saying nothing
- assertive: asking for what you want or saying how you feel in an honest and respectful way that does not impinge on another person's safety, dignity or well-being
- aggressive: asking for what you want or saying how you feel in an offensive, threatening or angry way.

Next, invite a member from each group in turn to place their soap character onto the thermometer in the place that they think best defines the character's behaviour. Encourage the young women to explain their decisions and ask them if they think the character gets what they want as a result of their behaviour. Go on to consider alternative ways that they could reach a positive conclusion.

Finally, invite each young woman to come up and write her own name on the anger thermometer, where she thinks her own behaviour ranks, when she is angry. Facilitate a discussion that looks at how passive or aggressive behaviour could become more assertive and set some individual goals.

5.14   Share/not share

This activity introduces the idea that there are parts of ourselves that we share with different people and bits that we choose to withhold. It can be used with young women individually or with small groups.

Aim

The aim is for the cards to promote discussion about what is appropriate to share, how we select and how this differs depending on our own 'comfort zones' and relationships.

You will need

- four pieces of card headed 'share with family', 'share with friends', 'share with partner' 'share with youth worker' and 'keep to self' (you will need one set for each group of three young women)
- a copy of the 'share/not share cards'
- information about counselling or support services.

How to do it

Before you start this activity make sure that you refer to the group ground rules and make sure everyone is comfortable with the boundaries that are in place. Revise if necessary.

Divide the young women into groups of three. Explain that this is basically a 'sorting' game; there is no wrong or right because it is up to them and how they feel about sharing personal information. Suggest that it may be that information is shared at different points in relationships, for example you may choose to share things with a friend that you have known for years but not with a new member of your class. Next give each group a set of headings and ask them to place them in front of the group in a line from left to right, then hand out the 'share/not share cards'.

Now, invite the young women to take it in turns to take a card, read it and consider whom they would share this information with. If they think that it is something that they would share then ask them to place it under the appropriate heading. If not then place it under the heading 'keep to self'.

Once all the cards are sorted facilitate a discussion around their decisions, without asking each group to feedback every choice they made. Look at the reasons that some things are kept private but suggest that sometimes we all need support or advice. Then ask whom they could go to for information or support if they were concerned and give out leaflets.

SHARE/NOT SHARE CARDS

My dad is not my real dad	I think I am pregnant	I have head lice	I want a baby
I plan to go to university	I don't fancy boys	My boyfriend wants to sleep with me – I'm not sure	I have slept with over ten boys
I have a criminal record	I think about death all the time	My dad is an alcoholic	I came top in my maths exam
I wish I was thinner	I make myself sick after food	I have tried cocaine	I am a virgin
I have inherited £5,000	I am being bullied at school	I am not sure what a French kiss is.	I have my period
My teacher told me I'm sexy	I wish my breasts were bigger	My partner hits me	I am not on the pill
I took the morning after pill	I have an alcoholic drink every day	I'm not always allowed to go out	My sisters keep stealing my stuff
I cheated in an exam	I don't know how to use condoms	I sometimes cut myself on my arm with a razor	I am ashamed of my family

5.15   Managing conflict

This is an activity that works best with an established group. However, make sure that there are no outstanding issues within the group that could lead to an argument and move the young women away from the task.

Aim

This activity provides an opportunity to explore potentially difficult situations and different ways to handle them.

You will need

- a set of the 'conflict cards' printed out and stuck onto pieces of A6 card.

How to do it

Seat the young women in a circle and explain that you are holding a set of 'conflict cards' that you are going to pass around the circle. Refer to any group rules and stress that this is an opportunity to share ideas, not to look at personal issues.

Pass the pack face down to the young woman on your right and ask her to take the first card, turn it over and read out loud the situation on the card that depicts some form of conflict situation. She should then offer a possible solution to manage the situation effectively.

Set the ground rules that only the person who is holding the card can talk first, but other ideas are welcome once this has happened. Offer the right to 'pass' or come back if anyone gets stuck.

Pass the cards around the circle until all the cards have been discussed. Pull together some 'top tips' on a flipchart sheet for further reference.

CONFLICT CARDS

Your friend constantly talks over the top of you and gets angry when you ask her to stop and let you finish.

Your mum shouts at you to do the washing up, but it is your sister's turn.

Your friend has been drinking heavily all night and is now starting to get into an argument with another girl.

Someone makes a rude comment about a member of your family.

Your boyfriend is in a bad mood and when you ask him what's wrong he shouts at you and kicks over a chair.

You walk past a group of girls in a club and notice that they keep staring at you.

You are babysitting and ask your younger brother to do something. He yells, 'You can't tell me what to do!'

You want to stay out with your friends till midnight but your stepdad is saying that you have to be in by 10.30 pm.

A young man that you went out with has been disrespecting you to his friends.

Your mate borrowed money off you but hasn't given it back. You really need it, but when you ask she just refuses.

You are on the train alone and a group of young men get on. They start making comments about the size of your breasts.

You are playing pool and winning. As you pot the black your opponent calls you a cheat.

Your mate gets into a fight with another young woman in the women's toilets and wants you to join in.

At school a teacher you don't like says something about you that makes the rest of the class laugh.

Chapter 6

Gender and Stereotypes

6.1   The sleepover

Aim

The aim of the game is for the young women to agree on six inspirational female 'guests' to invite for an imaginary sleepover. Guests can only go on the invite list if the whole group agree it.

You will need

- flipchart paper onto which you have already drawn a room and six 'beds'
- spare paper to negotiate on
- marker pens.

How to do it

Working in groups of no more than four set the young woman the task of drawing up the guest list for the best sleepover party ever! Explain that:

- It is a 'girls only' party.
- Guests can be chosen from anyone living or dead.
- The group must have reasons why the guest inspires, motivates or impresses that they can share.
- All group members must agree the invite.

Hand each group a flipchart sheet with the room layout on, marker pens and a spare sheet for working out the guest list on. Allow 20 minutes for the young women to suggest, negotiate and agree their guest list. The guest can then be allocated a bed on the plan.

When each group has made and agreed their final decisions, ask for a volunteer from each group to introduce their guest list. Each group then shares their sleepover plan and explains the reasons why these women have been chosen.

Review the process. How easy was it to agree guests? What makes a woman 'inspirational'? Are there any guests to make it on more than one list?

6.2   Exploring gender stereotypes

Aim

This small group activity encourages young women to explore both male and female gender stereotypes and considers ways to challenge them.

You will need

*   flipchart and markers.

How to do it

Divide the group into two halves: Group 1 and Group 2. Write 'Act like a man' at the top of one piece of flipchart paper and give this to Group 1, then write 'Be ladylike' on the top of the other and give to Group 2.

Ask the two groups to idea storm and write down responses to the headings. In turn invite feedback and then responses from each group. For example, Group 1 may have listed things such as 'Men don't cry, fight and are good at sport'. Is this true for all men? Where do these ideas of what is masculine behaviour come from?

Then consider Group 2's ideas of what it means to be 'ladylike', for example, caring, polite or tidy. At this point do not comment on any gender stereotypes, just acknowledge all the ideas given and take both sheets of flipchart paper and stick them up where everyone can see.

Now, take a thick black marker and draw a box around the ideas listed on each sheet. Explain that Box 1 is now labelled 'Act like a man' and Box 2, 'Be ladylike'. Suggest that inside the boxes are a list of attitudes and behaviours that reflect male and female stereotypes. Some may be true for some people, but none of them will be true for all men or all women. Ask the young women to consider if individuals are born with these gender differences, or if they are learnt. For example, are little girls born knowing how to care for babies and little boys how to mend things? How easy is it to break out of the 'box'? Conclude that many of the things inside the box are gender stereotypes with specific role expectations that people may feel pressured to conform to.

Move on to ask the young women where their own gender roles are learnt. For example, what messages have they received about what it means to be female, as they have grown up. This could include family and friends as well as the media, for example 'chick flicks'. Write these responses around the outside of the boxes, illustrating how these influences reinforce the wall of the stereotype box.

Finally, ask the young women, back in their groups, to consider what names or put-downs are directed at girls and women if they step out of the stereotype box?

How do these labels and names reinforce the stereotype box?

6.3   This is what I think

Aim

This is an activity that explores attitudes around stereotypes. It can be adapted and added to so that it reflects individual or group issues.

You will need

- a copy of the 'this is what I think' statements
- cards with 'agree', 'disagree' and 'don't know' written on them.

How to do it

Set up the room so that one side becomes the 'agree' area, the other 'disagree' and a central point between the two becomes the 'don't know' zone.

Introduce the room set-up to the girls and explain that you are going to read out a series of statements. Use all or some of those on the sheet adding any extra ones you can think of!

After each one invite the young women to move to the area of the room that corresponds best with their opinion regarding what has been said. Make sure that you stress that you want the group to be as honest as possible and that you expect differences of opinion.

Allow time between each statement for discussion and encourage the young women to question each other. Make sure that the young women standing in the middle zone have the opportunity to share their ideas too.

Finally ask if anyone wants to change places as a consequence of what they have heard.

THIS IS WHAT I THINK – STATEMENTS

1	Girls are more emotional and sensitive than boys.
2	Women who sleep with lots of men are 'slags'.
3	Women are much better at bringing up children than men.
4	If you get married it is not so important to have a career.
5	Thin women are more attractive/sexier than curvier girls.
6	All women want children at some point in their lives.
7	Most men would find it hard to have a female boss.
8	Women are natural homemakers and therefore much better at housework than men.
9	Men are better drivers than women.
10	Short hair makes you less attractive to men.
11	Women are less competitive than men.
12	Men really do prefer blondes.
13	The man should always ask the woman out first.
14	Mothers expect more of their daughters around the house than their sons.
15	You need to have a partner to be complete.

6.4   Career stereotypes

Aim

This activity opens up discussions to explore and challenge stereotypes around career opportunities.

You will need

- four sets of the 'career cards'
- paper and pens
- basic details about each of the professions, for example qualifications needed, average wage.

How to do it

In advance make up four sets of the career cards marked 'Librarian', 'Surgeon', 'Plumber', 'Firefighter', 'Web Designer' and 'Nursery Nurse'. Divide the young women into four groups and give each a set of cards, paper and pens. Write up the following questions and ask each group to look at the jobs on the cards and discuss the following for each one:

- Am I male or female?
- What age am I?
- What do I look like/what is my physical appearance?
- What sort of personality do I have?
- What qualifications do I have?
- What wages/salary do I get?

If the young women want to draw pictures instead of using words, then encourage them to illustrate their discussions. Facilitate feedback as each group shares their thoughts and ask where they got their information. Consider the sources – how accurate is this form of information likely to be? Does the media, for example newspapers and soap operas, reinforce any stereotypes? Are people's career choices informed by stereotypes about age, gender and social status?

Share the information that you have about the different career options and challenge any stereotypes.

CAREER CARDS

LIBRARIAN	SURGEON
PLUMBER	FIREFIGHTER
WEB DESIGNER	NURSERY NURSE

6.5   Whose job is it?

Aim

This is a small group activity to explore assumptions and the possible stereotypes surrounding jobs and career choices.

You will need

- sets of the 'job cards'
- flipchart and markers.

How to do it

Divide the young women into groups of four. Give each group a piece of flipchart paper and a marker. On the paper they should draw a large Venn diagram; the left hand circle should be labelled 'Male', the opposite circle 'Female' and the overlapping bit in the middle 'Either'.

Hand each group a pack of the job cards and ask them to categorise occupations under the headings.

Once all the cards have been laid invite the groups to feedback, encouraging discussion that considers:

- Do higher status jobs seem to end up in one pile rather than the other?
- Are some jobs dominated by one gender and not another?
- Are there any reasons why men or women should or should not do the jobs traditionally done by the opposite sex?

JOB CARDS

HAIRDRESSER	NURSE	PRIMARY SCHOOL TEACHER	IT CONSULTANT
CHILDMINDER	CLEANER	PLUMBER	COOK
BUTCHER	BUILDER	FOOTBALLER	INTERIOR DESIGNER
ACCOUNTANT	PHOTOGRAPHER	FILM DIRECTOR	FLORIST
POLICE INSPECTOR	MUSICIAN	DENTIST	VET
SCIENTIST	TRAVEL AGENT	CHEMIST	ELECTRICIAN
JOURNALIST	SOLICITOR	ELECTRICIAN	ARTIST
CAR SALES EXECUTIVE	FLIGHT ATTENDANT	SOCIAL WORKER	SALES ASSISTANT
HOLIDAY REP	MANAGER	FARMER	DOCTOR
SECRETARY	UNIVERSITY LECTURER	CARPENTER	CHEF

6.6   International Women's Day flags

Aim

To develop a celebration flag for International Women's Day.

You will need

- a large piece of white cotton (or an old sheet)
- fabric paint and brushes
- water pots
- fabric paint markers
- sequins, buttons, glitter, etc.
- paper and pens.

How to do it

This activity can be adapted to use with small or large groups of young women. Design one flag for a small group or several for a larger one.

First, suggest that flags have been used throughout history to represent groups of people, enabling others to see who they are and what they represent.

Now set the task, handing out paper and pens for the young women to design their flag on. Stress that the flag can have anything on it – pictures, symbols or simply colour; the only rule is that the design must be agreed by all and should represent as many groups of women as possible. Encourage the young women to think about their own cultural history, as well as considering women in the wider world.

Once the design has been agreed give out the fabric and fabric paints for the young women to transfer the design onto fabric.

When the flag is finished and dry hang it up as a symbol of womankind around the world.

6.7   Gender facts – true or false?

Aim

This quick quiz offers facts and promotes discussion about gender and inequality.

You will need

- the 'gender facts – true or false?' sheet
- paper and pens.

How to do it

Give out pens and paper to each member of the group. Explain that you are going to read out a series of 'facts'. For each one, the young women should write either 'true' or 'false', depending on whether they think the fact is real or not.

Go through the answers, raising points to discuss and encouraging questions. The young woman with the most correct answers wins the quiz. Review the process, considering the facts and drawing out conclusions around gender and any inequalities the group perceive.

GENDER FACTS – TRUE OR FALSE?[3]

1	Eight out of ten men and women in England said that watching TV was their favourite leisure activity in 2007.	True.
2	Overall, there are slightly more females than males in the world.	False – for the first time since World War II there are slightly fewer.
3	On average, women spend over 2 hours 30 minutes a day doing housework, cooking, washing up, cleaning and ironing.	True – according to the 2004 Lifestyle Survey. This compares with 1 hour 30 minutes for males.
4	The life expectancy from birth in the UK is 77.2 years for males and 81.6 for females.	True.
5	In 2001 the average age to get married for the first time in England was 27 for men and 24 for women.	False – in 2001 it was 30 for men and 28 for women. In 1971 it was 24 for men and 22 for women.
6	Women head eight out of ten single-parent families in the UK.	False – nine out of ten.

---

3   Information is taken from the National Statistics Office's 'Focus on Gender' findings in 2008 (www.statistics.gov.uk).

7	There are around 17 times as many men as women in prisons.	True.
8	Girls generally perform better than boys at GCSE in the UK.	True – in 2005/06, 64 per cent of girls achieved five or more GCSE grades A*–C, compared with 54 per cent of boys.
9	The average woman makes 314 shopping trips a year.	False – 243 trips, including food and family shopping, which women do more of.
10	In the UK more men than women own their own homes.	True – in 2006 more than three-quarters of men owned their home compared with three-fifths of women.
11	In 2008 more women had jobs than men.	False – a greater proportion of men than women of working age in the UK were in employment in 2008.
12	More men than women drink over the recommended weekly safe drinking limit.	True – in 2007, 24 per cent of men and 13 per cent of women drank over the weekly recommendations (21 units for men and 14 units for women).

6.8   Women in parliament

Aim

This activity provides information and provokes debate around women and politics.

You will need

- the 'true/false sheet'
- two A4 cards – one marked 'true', the other 'false'.

How to do it

Place the card marked 'true' at one end of the room and the card marked 'false' at the other. Introduce the activity by explaining that you are going to read out a series of statements. For each you want the young women to move to either the 'true' area of the room or the 'false' area, depending on what they think. Stress that it is a personal response that you want and that they should go with what they think or know.

Go through the list giving the answers as you go and allowing time for questions or debate.

If you are based outside of the UK, you could devise your own list of true/false statements about women in international politics for the young women to consider.

TRUE/FALSE SHEET[4]

1	In the early 1990s there were more MPs in the House of Commons called John than there were women MPs.	True.
2	In 1918 women won the right to vote, but only over the age of 21.	False – in 1918 men could vote at the age of 21 but women had to wait until they were 30.
3	Only 69 per cent of women voted in the last General Election.	False – only 59 per cent of women voted in the 2005 General Election.
4	Diane Abbott was the first black female MP.	True – elected in 1987.
5	Women aged 55 and over are more likely to vote than young women under 24.	True – according to statistics from the last General Election.
6	Margaret Thatcher was the second female British Prime Minister.	False – so far she is the only one. She was first elected Prime Minister in 1979.
7	The Isle of Man, the first country in the world to introduce votes for women, lowered the official voting age to 16 in 2006.	True – UK Youth Parliament is currently campaigning for everyone to have the vote at 16.
8	Jacqui Smith became Britain's first female Home Secretary in June 2007.	True.

4   Information is taken from the following websites: www.bbc.co.uk, www.statistics.gov.uk, www.equalities. gov.uk, www.ukyouthparliament.org.uk.

6.9   Role models activity

This is a group activity that is fun and can be used as a group 'tool' for future activities.

Aim

To design a pack of playing cards that depicts role models who are important to the group and promote discussions about positive role models for young women.

You will need

- 52 A6 cards (four different colours, 13 of each colour)
- black and red marker pens
- at least 52 pictures of possible role models
- glue.

How to do it

Divide the group into four and explain that the task is to design a deck of playing cards that depicts inspirational role models for young women. Assign each group a suit – Diamonds, Spades, Hearts or Clubs.

Give each group a set of pictures to look through and discuss. Point out that just because the picture is included you are not necessarily identifying these women as positive role models – it is up to the group to decide. Additionally, they can add their own role models or heroes. Thirteen women can be chosen to represent the different cards, for example the Queen of Hearts or the Ace of Clubs. Explain that everyone in the group must agree a nominee before she is stuck onto one of the A6 cards.

Once each group has finished invite them in turn to share their choices and explain why they think that this person is a role model for young women. You should then have a deck of playing cards that the group can use for other activities.

This can be developed into a discussion; for example, what do young women feel about including suggestions for role models that perpetuate stereotypes?

Ideas for role models

- Lady Gaga
- Lily Allen
- Margaret Thatcher
- Kate Moss
- Princess Diana
- Lindsay Lohan
- Jordan
- Dame Tanni Grey-Thompson
- Kylie
- Ellen DeGeneres
- Oprah Winfrey
- Nicole Kidman
- Meryl Streep
- Mother Teresa
- Marilyn Monroe
- Mary Seacole

- Beyoncé Knowles
- Victoria Beckham
- Angelina Jolie
- Madonna
- Dawn French
- Sarah Jessica Parker
- Venus Williams
- Emmeline Pankhurst
- Davina McCall
- Paris Hilton
- Michelle Obama
- Hilary Clinton
- Mariah Carey
- Shakira
- Jennifer Aniston
- HRH Queen Elizabeth II

Chapter 7

Endings

7.1   Positive thoughts

This evaluation encourages the young women to think about the role that other group members have played in making the session a success for them.

Aim

To encourage the group to identify positive attributes in each other.

You will need

* nothing!

How to do it

Ask the young women to sit down in a wide circle.

Explain that what you would like them to do is to say 'goodbye' and one positive thing to the person on their left and right in the circle.

Stress that only positive comments are welcome and make sure no one is left out or feels isolated. Include yourself and your co-worker in the process.

So for example, 'Goodbye Donna, I though you worked really hard in our team game' or 'Goodbye Millie, thanks for listening to me'.

Finally, go around the circle again and ask the young women to say one positive thing about the group itself.

7.2   The self-esteem gauntlet

This activity is great to use with any size of group and promotes good feelings at the end of a session.

Aim

To promote self-esteem and the ability to give and receive compliments.

You will need

- nothing!

How to do it

Form two lines with the young women facing each other. Have one person walk or skip in between the two lines and 'run' the gauntlet.

As each young woman walks through the line, others pat her on the back, or give her a hug, offer positive comments, or smile. Encourage each young woman to go through the gauntlet slowly and to listen to the words and gestures given to her.

Finish the activity by giving each other a round of applause.

7.3   Letter to self

Aim

To reinforce learning and remind young women of the goals they set themselves.

You will need

- a plain postcard for each group member with a stamp on it
- pens.

How to do it

Hand out a postcard and pen to each young woman in the group.

Ask the young women to spend a couple of minutes thinking about what they have learnt about themselves, each other and the goals they have set themselves as a result of their time with you.

When they are ready ask the young women to write, on the blank side of the postcard, a letter to themselves reminding themselves of any changes they want to make as a consequence of the group, things that they have learnt or any goals that they have set.

On the other side they should write their name and address before handing the postcards back to you.

Make a note in your diary of the date in a month's time and then post the cards as a reminder/reinforcement on that day to the young women.

7.4   Day at the beach

This ending session can be adapted to use with any group. Other themes could be Christmas or a field of flowers.

Aim

To create a safe, calming environment for the young women to reflect on their session with you and relax.

You will need

- a CD player
- a CD with soft music and sounds of ocean waves
- a big hand fan or a piece of cardboard to use as a fan
- different aromas to burn or scented candles to evoke a summer beach
- a shell for each young woman.

How to do it

Start with the young women sitting in a circle on the floor, with the music playing softly in the background.

Outline the activity to the group and ask each of them to begin to relax by stretching their arms and circling their head to release any tension in their neck and let their breathing slow down.

Then ask the women to lie down, if they feel comfortable doing this, and to close their eyes. Dim any lights, light the candles or oil burners and turn on the CD. This should include music but also have sounds of waves breaking on the shore and other seaside sounds, such as gulls. Allow time for the young women to get used to the music playing and encourage them to relax their bodies completely.

Begin by saying that you are going to lead them on a journey to total relaxation and ask them to picture in their mind a place they have been or can imagine that is special by the seaside. Start off the journey by asking questions gently about where they are, for example, 'Can you see the sea? Look how blue the water is today. Feel the sun on your face and relax your facial muscles as it starts to warm you.' Continue from the beach onto an imaginary boat or lead them into the water, whatever you think is appropriate.

Keep going until everyone has relaxed entirely and then start to slowly bring the session to a close by saying that the sun is now going down and that you are going to gradually bring them back to the present time.

Wind the scenario down and invite the young women to open their eyes and slowly sit up. Once the whole group is sitting ask them to slowly stand again and stretch their body until they have their arms above their heads.

Thank everyone and lead a round of applause for the whole group and close.

7.5   Presentations

This is appropriate to use at the final session of a group or with a group who know each other well.

Aim

To devise and share presentations about each other's contribution to the group.

You will need

- a copy of the 'presentation sheet' for each group member
- pens.

How to do it

This is an activity to use to close a group at the end of their time together using positive reinforcement and individual praise.

Allocate each young woman a group member about whom they will develop a presentation, using the sheet. Make sure you refer to any group contract before you start and stress that only positive comments are welcome.

Hand out the sheets and allow about ten minutes for the young women to complete them.

Once everyone has prepared their presentation invite the young women to form a seated circle and ask them to share their presentations in turn. Lead a round of applause after each one and thank the presenter.

Close by asking the circle to stand and shake hands with the person to their left and right before breaking up the group.

PRESENTATION SHEET

Name	
Description of who they are	
One thing they brought to the group	
How you see them in the future	
Positive words you have for them	
Wishing them well for the future	

7.6   Action planning for positive change

This is shown as a paired activity but with more support you could use it for individuals too.

Aim

This is an activity to reinforce learning and to focus on goals.

You will need

- a copy of the 'action planning sheet' for each person
- pens.

How to do it

Ask the young women to divide themselves into pairs for this activity.

Hand out an 'action planning sheet' and a pen to each young woman. Allow a few minutes for individual reading and thinking about the sheet and then ask the young women to move into their pairs to work on the task.

Encourage them to work on the sheets, taking it in turns to share goals and support and listen to their partner. Stress that you are there to offer additional support if anyone gets really stuck or needs to ask questions that their partner can't answer.

Once everyone has completed their action plan explain that these are personal and that the young women should take them home with them to refer to later. Agree review dates when they should look at their plan and review how it has gone and add anything else that needs to be noted.

ACTION PLANNING SHEET

NAME	
WHAT DO I WANT?	1.
	2.
	3.
WHAT STOPS ME?	
HOW WILL I GET WHAT I WANT?	1.
	2.
	3.
BY WHEN?	
REVIEW AND UPDATE	Date
	Date

7.7   Treasured comments

Aim

The aim of this review is to experience giving and receiving positive comments by creating 'treasure boxes'.

You will need

- an envelope per person with a picture of a treasure chest stuck onto it
- coloured paper cut into strips to fit into the envelopes
- pens.

How to do it

Give each member of the group a 'treasure chest' and ask them to write their name on it. Explain that this treasure chest will contain all sorts of positive messages to them by the end of the activity.

Next, provide each young woman with enough brightly coloured paper strips to write a message to each member of the group. Encourage everyone to spend time thinking of something positive to say about each other. They should then write that positive message on one of the coloured strips.

When everyone has finished writing their comments, they should walk around and put their messages in one another's envelopes. At the end of the activity, each young person will have a 'treasured comments chest' to read on their own.

7.8   Hand curtain

This is a really effective way to end a group, but make sure you have space to display it properly.

Aim

To create a visual review of the group's learning and experiences.

You will need

- one A4 sheet of thin card for each young woman and a length of thin string
- felt-tip pens
- scissors
- hole punch
- drawing pins.

How to do it

Each member of the group takes a sheet of card and a pen and draws around their hand, cutting it out to make a personal template.

Invite each young woman to write something that they have learnt from your group session. This can be something factual such as 'I did not realise that cocaine is a Class A drug', or something around attitudes and values, for example 'I feel more confident now!'

On the other side ask the young women to write down the activity/experience that they enjoyed the most.

When everyone has made a statement and identified a favourite part of the work, hand around the hole punch and ask that they punch a single hole into their card hand. It doesn't matter too much where but it should be around the edge otherwise it won't hang properly later.

Give each young woman a length of string and ask her to attach it to the hand.

As a group you can now display the evaluations using the drawing pins to create a curtain of 'hands'.

7.9   Positive footsteps

This activity works particularly well with groups of 12 or more, as it is a visual representation of everyone taking part.

Aim

To close the group in a positive way.

You will need

- two footprint cards for each group member
- marker pens
- stamped addressed envelopes
- music.

How to do it

BEFORE THE SESSION

Using coloured card, make footprint shaped cards – the easiest way is to make a template by drawing around your own foot! That way all the cards will be the same size. Find envelopes that the footprint card will fit into and write the names and addresses of all the young women in the group on them with a stamp ready for use.

AT THE SESSION

At the end of the group session form a seated circle and hand each young woman a footprint card and a marker pen. Ask the young women to think and then write a positive message about a member of the group on each card. If you think this may result in someone being left out, orchestrate it so that you write names on the cards first.

Play the music – this should be up-tempo and inspirational – and invite the young women to place the cards on the floor leading to the door before returning to their seats.

Lead the group across the footprint cards to leave the session stopping to read the messages as they go.

Finally, collect up the footprints and place in the appropriate envelopes and post to the young women in a week's time as a reminder of the session.

7.10   One memory...

This is a circle time activity that should be fun and raise a few laughs to end the session on a positive note.

Aim

To reinforce positive experiences within the group.

You will need

- nothing!

How to do it

Ask the young women to sit in a large circle so that they can see each other. If you haven't used circle time before set the ground rules that everyone can speak in the circle but no one can talk when someone else is talking. Refer to any group contract if appropriate to reinforce safety in the group.

Start the round off yourself by saying, 'One memory I will take away from this group is...' Make sure it is something positive you are recalling and something that everyone will remember.

Invite the young woman sitting next to you to continue with her memory and keep going until everyone has had a turn in sharing something.

Lead a round of applause for everyone and thank the young women for their contributions and close.

7.11   Positive steps circle

This circle time activity encourages the young women to think about something that they have learnt through the time spent in the group and to identify something positive that they will do because of it for the future.

Aim

To encourage the young women to identify and plan positive actions that they can take.

You will need

- nothing!

How to do it

Ask the young women to sit down in a wide circle.

Explain that what you would like them to do is to say 'goodbye' to the group and identify one positive 'step' that they are going to make as a direct result of the work that they have done in the session. Encourage the young women to make these realistic and to recognise the value of making small, achievable steps.

So for example, 'Goodbye, I am going to stop eating chocolate for one week.'

Finally, go around the circle again and ask the young women to close the session by saying one positive thing about the group itself.

Useful Websites

These organisations offer information about topics relating to young women and can be useful for updating legislation and knowledge. The author can take no responsibility for the contents and the views expressed are not necessarily shared or endorsed because they are included.

www.advocatesforyouth.org
Advocates for Youth champions efforts that help young people make informed and responsible decisions about their reproductive and sexual health.

www.bbc.co.uk/switch/surgery/advice/
'The Surgery' BBC site has lots of useful information, tips, advice, quizzes and Top 10s. There are also separate A–Zs of life for boys and girls, covering drugs, sex, relationships, school and work.

www.brook.org.uk
The Brook provides free, confidential sex advice and contraception to young people.

www.bullying.co.uk
The Bullying UK website provides help and advice on bullying issues and resource ideas.

www.byc.org.uk
The British Youth Council website represents the views of young people aged 16–25 in the UK.

www.campaignforrealbeauty.co.uk
Dove's website includes a section on their Campaign for Real Beauty.

www.condomessentialwear.co.uk

This website gives information about contraception and STIs and a free, confidential helpline.

www.cyh.com

The Children, Youth and Women's Health Service (CYWHS) promotes the health, well-being and development of children, young people and families across South Australia.

www.doh.gov.uk

The UK government website for the Department of Health offers information about a wide range of health related issues including alcohol, drugs and sexual health.

www.drugscope.org.uk

DrugScope is a UK charity providing up-to-date information on drug issues.

www.equalities.gov.uk

The Government Equalities Office has responsibility within Government for equality strategy and legislation and takes the lead on issues relating to women, sexual orientation and transgender equality matters.

www.fpa.org.uk

The Family Planning Association offers information, a guide to contraception and sexual health.

www.headspace.org.au

Headspace provides mental and health well-being support, information and services to young people and their families across Australia.

www.likeitis.org.uk

The Like It Is website has an Australian and UK portal. The site offers comprehensive information about sexual heath issues: contraception, illness, peer pressure, puberty, sexuality and more.

www.need2know.co.uk/health

The need2know website contains advice on relationships, student life, money troubles, travel and leisure, plus a wide range of tips and resources on a wide range of issues.

www.now.org

The National Organization for Women (NOW) is the largest organisation of feminist activists in the United States. NOW's goal is to take action to bring about equality for all women.

www.nya.org.uk

This is the website for the UK National Youth Agency. The NYA works in partnership with a wide range of public, private and voluntary sector organisations to support and improve services for young people.

www.queeryouth.org.uk

The Queer Youth Network was founded by a collection of local gay youth groups that came together to form a regional network supporting the needs of local LGBT (lesbian, gay, bisexual and transgender) young people. It also has a linked site in Australia.

www.suzylamplugh.org

The Suzy Lamplugh Trust's website provides information and advice on personal safety.

www.talktofrank.com

The FRANK website offers drugs information and support.

www.ukyouth.org

UK Youth is a UK charity that develops and promotes innovative non-formal education programmes for and with young people.

www.womensaid.org.uk

The Women's Aid Federation of England (Women's Aid) is the national charity working to end domestic violence against women and children.

www.yjb.gov.uk

The website of the Youth Justice Board for England and Wales (YJB) offers information and updates on the laws and orders relating to young people.

www.ywca.org

The YWCA (Young Women's Christian Association) is the oldest and largest multicultural women's association in the world.